365
Glasses of
Wine

365 Glasses of Wine

Helen Brown

Reading Stones Publishing

Copyright © 2020; Helen Brown.

ISBN: Softcover: 978-0-6488143-4-4
         eBook: 978-0-6488143-5-1

All rights reserved. No part of this book may be reproduced or transmitted in any form or by any means, electronic or mechanical, including photocopying, recording, or by any information storage and retrieval system, without permission in writing from the copyright owner.

Scripture quotations marked KJV are from the Holy Bible, King James Version (Authorized Version). First published in 1611. Quoted from the KJV Classic Reference Bible, Copyright © 1983 by The Zondervan Corporation.

Scripture quotations marked NLT are taken from the Holy Bible, New Living Translation, copyright © 1996, 2004, 2007. Used by permission of Tyndale House Publishers, Inc. Carol Stream, Illinois 60188. All rights reserved.

Scripture quotations marked HCSB are taken from the Holman Christian Standard Bible ®, Used by Permission HCSB ©1999,2000,2002,2003,2009 Holman Bible Publishers. Holman Christian Standard Bible ®, Holman CSB ®, and HCSB ® are federally registered trademarks of Holman Bible Publishers.

Any people depicted in stock imagery provided by Shutterstock are models, and such images are being used for illustrative purposes only.
www.shutterstock.com.

First published 2017
This edition published 2020

Published by: Reading Stones Publishing
Helen Brown and Wendy Wood
Hbrown19561@gmail.com
www.woodwendy1982.wixsite.com/readingstones

Cover design: Wendy Wood

To order additional copies of this book, contact the publisher at:
Glenburnie homestead
212 Glenburnie Rd
Rob Roy NSW 2360
Hbrown19561@gmail.com

1

I was too tired to stay up until midnight. It's the beginning of a new year. I woke up after a full night's sleep. The sky stretched out above me all the way to the horizon, just like the year before me stretches out from January to December. I observed that there were a number of clouds floating above me. However, I knew that they could disappear altogether, or they might even build into great storm clouds.

As I face my new year, I too, have some clouds gathering in the sky. These, like the real ones, could disappear and evaporate or they could develop into storm clouds, bringing with them tears, sorrow, and grief. The year is still new and I cannot predict what is going to happen but I do know that the Son is the shining light in my life, just like the sun is the most powerful light in the sky; He is the most powerful source of strength, courage, and inspiration in my life. So, let the New Year begin.

"Have not I commanded thee? Be strong and of a good courage; be not afraid, neither be thou dismayed: for the LORD thy God *is* with thee whithersoever thou goest." Joshua 1:9

Prayer: Lord, I need to listen to your word and not only take it to heart but put it into practice. Practice makes perfect they say.

2

If I'm honest, I'm a little scared of routine. It seems to me that if you do the same thing every day, in the same order and at the same time, life could get very boring. There is a saying that says, "variety is the spice of life". I have tried over the years, not even just as a New Year's resolution, to try and get myself into a routine. They tell me that it helps reduce stress. Each time I tried, it would work for a day or two and then I, or the kids, would get sick and the routine went out the window.

As a farmers' wife, there are always things happening that will throw a spanner in the works. No matter what is going on in my house there is one thing that I must always keep in my routine. That is talking to God, regardless of where and when with my eyes opened and my thoughts only. It helps to keep me less stressed, better than any solid routine could.

"Pray without ceasing." 1 Thessalonians 5:17.

<u>*Prayer:*</u> Lord, thank you for listening to me all the time.

 3

I often have fellowship with the ladies of our Presbyterian Women's Association group in my hometown. These ladies have been my prayer partners for the last twenty years. They have watched me struggle with the everyday issues of raising a family within the boundaries of the farming world.

This group has also been a framework that has helped develop many of the skills that I have. As a member of this group, I have been able to advance my speaking, administration and writing talents. Most of them would be totally unaware of their influence on me or anyone else.

"And whatsoever ye do, do *it* heartily, as to the Lord, and not unto men;" Colossians 3:23 and "With good will doing service, as to the Lord, and not to men:" Ephesians 6:7

<u>*Prayer:*</u> I thank you for all those people that you have sent to encourage me.

 4

I was thinking back to when the year 2000 was the New Year. I thought about how many people were so fearful of what the new millennium would mean for humanity. Now here we are so many years later and life is still happening in much the same way as it had in the last century. Yes, we have seen loss, destruction, and wars but we saw those things in the previous century as well. Yet, looking back I can see God's faithfulness at work.

"The LORD shall preserve thee from all evil: he shall preserve thy soul."
Psalm 121:7.

Prayer: Lord, help me to remember that you are there always and when I feel afraid all I need to do is look to you.

5

As each year comes and goes, I learn more and more about God's love and care, not only for me but for all of humanity. Yes, it's hard to see sometimes, especially when bad things happen, but He has a plan and He will not let that plan go astray. He drew that plan up long before He created the world and when it is completed, He will still be there in control.

"I am Alpha and Omega, the beginning and the end, the first and the last." Revelation 22:13.

Prayer: Thank you, Lord, that you are who you are, every unchanging.

6

There were lots of little moments of fear while I was sick, more than little some were, in fact, rather large as I faced surgery. Handing control to the doctor is very difficult. If anything goes wrong, there will be nothing that I will be able to do to help myself or to fix the situation. I am completely in their hands.

We often say that we want to allow God to have complete control of our lives but I was suddenly faced with realizing just what that really meant. If I can put my life into the hands of the doctor, then I should be able to trust that God is going to fix it and I should keep my hands off the problem as hard as that may be.

"For I the LORD thy God will hold thy right hand, saying unto thee, Fear not; I will help thee." Isaiah 41:13.

Prayer: Lord, please may I trust you to control my life.

 7

My husband and I were married on my Mum and Dad's 22nd Wedding Anniversary. I'm not going to kid around and tell you that we lived happily ever after once the wedding was over. As much as that's how it's supposed to happen, that is, the trials and tribulations are in the lead up to the wedding and then a couple get married and they walk off into the sunset, dancing into an eternity of wedded bliss. What I am going to tell you is; we have had more downs than ups, sickness, miscarriages, financial stress, and grief have all been a very large part of all our years.

The Bible reading at our ceremony was 1 Corinthians 13:1- 13. While I have often failed to live up to the standards set down in this passage, God has never failed me.

"Charity never faileth: but whether there be prophecies, they shall fail; whether there be tongues, they shall cease; whether there be knowledge, it shall vanish away." 1 Corinthians 13:8.

Prayer: Thank you, Lord, for never failing to love me.

8

My children love reading books that have a number of stories, a series. I was thinking about how life is also like a book series. This is where I realized that life is a "series" - our children will have their own stories as they move on into the future. Our stories are not just carried on by our children they can also be carried on by the people we influence through our work, charity, and recreation. Yes, life is a series of sorts and will continue until the day when Jesus returns. Then we will start our final story that will go on forever and forever and there will be no more 'afters'.

"And I saw a new Heaven and a new earth: for the first Heaven and the first earth were passed away; and there was no more sea." Revelation 21:1.

Prayer: Thank you for all the people who you have made part of my life series.

 # 9

Most moments are ordinary. As each second ticks by, it is rare for something spectacular to happen. Yet in amongst all those moments, there will be some that will stand out as the beginning of something extraordinary. A moment when something happened that begins a great journey into a new life, new career, or new lifestyle. Often, we will only recognize that special moment as we look back on the journey that we have been travelling for some time. We won't be at the end of it but will have travelled far enough from the beginning to be able to see that moment as something spectacular.

Of course, there is one moment in everyone's journey that will always mark the beginning of a new life, an eternal life. That moment is when we leave our earthly bodies and exchange them for the eternal one. However, what we have done with all those ordinary moments on earth, no matter how many of them there are, will determine where we will spend that eternal life.

"But of that day and *that* hour knoweth no man, no, not the angels which are in heaven, neither the Son, but the Father." Mark 13:32.

Prayer: Lord, guide my moments so that my life will have eternal value.

 10

A black computer screen brings my anger pretty close to the surface. Yes, it is a silly thing to get angry over, I know. Such things as people being treated badly and corrupt dealings are much more distressing. The hope of knowing that my computer can be fixed helps me to stay reasonably calm. That is the hope that we have as Christians, one-day God will fix it, on that day when Jesus returns. He will create a new perfect Heaven and earth and no one will be angry.

"Be ye angry, and sin not: let not the sun go down upon your wrath:" Ephesians 4:26.

Prayer: Lord, help me to remember that one day you will fix all that is wrong.

11

I was listening to the tales of the manufacture, specifically, of chocolate and wine, regarding the ghastly facts of bugs and snakes while sitting at the dinner table. I was at the point where I was having trouble keeping my food down when I thought about how life can be filled with unsavoury moments and great danger.

These things are just a part of life. No matter how careful we are, we will always find ourselves facing these things and the consequences will often mean that we have to move through the process of grief.

However, just like the Chocolate and Wine, we will be transformed into something that is precious.

"And we know that all things work together for good to them that love God, to them who are the called according to his purpose." Romans 8:28.

Prayer: Lord, thank you for making something good out of my ugliness.

12

Some people will try and tell us that we are only very smart animals. Not only do we differ from the four-legged animal variety in the possession of a soul but even when we are being driven, we are going to a point of our choosing. It is something that we have a say in. Some people will tell you that they didn't have a say in what they are doing but at some point they did.

Sheep, cattle, horses, or goats do not have a choice in their destination. They are being pushed into a new paddock or yard so they can get a better feed if they are not being driven to market. Unlike those sheep, we can take heed of the word of God and follow Him against the masses.

"All we like sheep have gone astray; we have turned everyone to his own way, and the LORD hath laid on him the iniquity of us all." Isaiah 53:6.

Prayer: Lord, I thank you that you made us in your likeness, not just another animal.

13

As we wake up each day, we never know what will be part of it. Some things will always be the same, such as the sun will rise and set, the moon will appear according to its cycle. They will be there even if we cannot see through barriers a such as a building's roof, the clouds or smog. It will not matter how things change or how fast they change and it will not matter if they change for the better or for worse, Jesus will be there,

No matter what happens we know there is one person that will always remain the same. Jesus!

"Jesus Christ the same yesterday and today and forever." Hebrews 13:8.

Prayer: I thank you for always being the same.

 14

The truth is that all the things that I find beautiful are relative. A rainy day is always beautiful to a farmer after three years of drought. A sunny day will be beautiful after a week of rain and floods. A fire is beautiful in winter, not so in summer.

A baby is always beautiful to their parents. A building will be beautiful to the Architect regardless of what I think of it. When people are kind to each other we say that it is a beautiful thing because it is good. When God created the earth, (Genesis 1) He looked at what He created at the end of each day and said: "it was good".

"In the eyes of God, I am beautiful, no matter what I look like because God tells me that "... I am fearfully and wonderfully made; marvellous are thy works..." (Psalm 139:14)

Prayer: Thank you God that you made lots of things that are good and therefore beautiful.

15

While having a shower one morning, I thought about beauty being skin deep, and in the eyes of the beholder, I asked God to show me something different. When we have finished our showers, we feel fresh, clean, revitalized, and ready for work. But isn't this exactly what happens when our sins are washed away by the sacrifice of Jesus on the cross. We feel fresh, clean, revitalized, and ready for work and a lot warmer towards the people around us.

"If we confess our sins, he is faithful and just to forgive us *our* sins, and to cleanse us from all unrighteousness." 1 John 1:9.

Prayer: Lord, I thank you for making me clean all the way through.

16

As I look at the papers strewn all over the other side of my bed one afternoon, a sigh escaped. Some people will tell you that in order to have the correct mindset about your work you should dress and set up your workplace as if you are going to the office. Others will tell you that if you want to sleep well, then your bed should be exclusively for sleeping. This would mean that I break all these rules most of the time. This doesn't mean that I ignore all the other jobs that need to be done. They still get completed, I get to enjoy the view through the window while I write and work at the most unsavoury jobs on my agenda.

I am glad that God allows me to work in this way and bless what I do, however small, and inadequate I feel about it.

"For the LORD thy God hath blessed thee in all the works of thy hand: he knoweth thy walking through this great wilderness:" Deuteronomy 2:7.

Prayer: Lord, I thank you that I can work for you in all the most unlikely places, even my bed.

⛾ 17

My granddaughter was so excited. She was having her first "big girl" sleepover at grandmas. Being a "big girl" meant that she would get to spend the night without mum and dad. She was striking out on her own for the first time. I'm pretty sure that the experience was very different to what she had expected but it didn't stop her from asking to do it again.

This is often our own experience in life, isn't it? We have expectations as to what a particular career, relationships or even outing might be like. We can often be sure that God has led us in a particular direction. Of course, what God has in mind is often very different to that preconceived idea. It's not an easy thing to understand but with the help of the Holy Spirit, it can be done.

"But the Comforter, *which is* the Holy Ghost, whom the Father will send in my name, he shall teach you all things, and bring all things to your remembrance, whatsoever I have said unto you." John 14:26.

Prayer: Lord, give me the insight to see things differently to what I expect.

⛾ 18

We often want life to be black and white. That would mean that there is a very definite right and wrong about how everyone should live. One thing that annoys me is the need, that so many people have, to tell everyone what they need to do! If life was black and white, it would be a case of one size fits all. You and I know that this just isn't the case.

God has made us as individuals. Like most black and white photos that means that there are many grey areas along our life's road. What might work for me may not necessarily work for others. That does not mean that I am right or wrong, just different.

> "Even as I please all *men* in all *things*, not seeking mine own profit, but the *profit* of many, that they may be saved." 1 Corinthians 10:33.

Prayer: Lord, please help us to focus on you only.

19

The rules in our society used to be very much a black and white issue. Something was either right or wrong, but only according to those that set the rules. There was, quite often, a lack of understanding applied to the circumstances of those to whom the rules were applied. Particularly in regard to wrongdoing. Today there seems to be a greater expansion of that grey area. This has been brought about supposedly because those applying the laws of the land are taking into consideration the environmental influences that may have contributed to the situation. This leaves many of us finding it very hard to understand the consequences faced by those who commit crimes. We are told in the bible that one day God will decide for a final time what is right and what is wrong as in Matthew 25:31-46.

> "These will go away into eternal punishment, but the righteous into life eternal." Matthew 25:46.

Prayer: Lord, I thank you for telling us what is right and wrong in your word.

♀ 20

As I walked past a garden, I spotted a beautiful mauve Iris in a bed that didn't have a lot of other brightly coloured plants in it, so the Iris stood out and grabbed my attention.

I would like to stand out in a world that is a bit dull and sad. I want to be able to bring some joy and encouragement to people around me. I know that there are days when I would rather moan than smile, but I hope that I will remember that flower, and smile instead, bringing beauty to someone else.

"Wherefore comfort yourselves together, and edify one another, even as also ye do." 1 Thessalonians 5:11.

Prayer: Lord, may I smile instead of moan and make somebody's day better.

♀ 21

When I am feeling blue, I like to sit in the sunshine and look at the bright blue sky. I am very blessed to only suffer from a mild form of depression; unlike some other people I know. Yes, I sometimes think it is a curse, but I have learned that there are some things that will make me feel down (grey skies and dark places) and some things that will lift my spirits.

I have also learned that God is still with me, even when I am feeling down. How do I know this? I know this because He has promised:

"For he hath said, I will never leave thee, nor forsake thee. So that we may boldly say, The Lord *is* my helper, and I will not fear what man shall do unto me." Hebrews 13:5b-6.

Prayer: Thank you God that I am alive and I have blue skies that lift my spirits.

22

I was borrowed, one day, to babysit my great grandson. I realized that if we borrow, someone has to lend. It's not the opposite of borrow but goes hand in hand with it. The thing about something being borrowed is that you only have possession of the article for a short period of time. It is often said that our children are lent to us, not given. We bring home our newborn babies and there are times when we think that this parenting job is going to go on forever. Then one day, we watch our children walk out the door and realize that our time with them is over. They have their own lives, our role as parents have shifted into a different gear in this thing called life.

> "Whereas ye know not what shall be on the morrow. For what is your life? It is even a vapour, that appeareth for a little time, and then vanisheth away." James 4:14.

Challenge: Life here is actually borrowed time. We are here for such a short while, may we make the most of it by serving God faithfully.

23

Lightning is so bright, that we can often see it from miles/kilometres away. As a child, I remember counting the seconds between seeing the lightning and hearing the thunder to roughly work out how far away the storm was. Sometimes the storms made me afraid.

Some angels are said to shine so brightly, so much so that they frighten people when they appear, which meant that they had to tell humans not to be afraid, examples of this are seen when the angel appeared to Mary, and the shepherds, and when Jesus went up onto the mountain and was transfigured.

> "And after six days Jesus taketh Peter, James, and John his brother and bringeth them up into a high mountain apart, and was transfigured

before them and his face did shine as the sun and his raiment was white as the light" Matthew 17:1-2.

<u>*Challenge:*</u> May we shine for God and help others to not be afraid.

 **24**

As I thought about Candy, and I had to think hard, I wondered about other things that we like to sweeten. It is often distasteful for us to be confronted by someone who is telling us some unpleasant truth about ourselves, or, where we have hurt someone, intentional or not, it makes us uncomfortable. That's why we often tell people that the truth is a tough pill to swallow.

I also thought about how Nathan rebuked David. How he was able to tell David the truth in a loving and sweetened way (2 Samuel 12). When we have to confront people about challenging issues, do we go to God first and ask Him to guide us in how we approach someone? I have known some people who will just wade in boots and all without giving any consideration to making their words sweet.

"This is my commandment: That ye love one another, as I have loved you." John 15:12.

<u>*Challenge:*</u> Let's try and add some sweetness when telling people difficult things and not just dish up nasty tasting medicine.

25

In our lives, we often find that we feel as if we are wading in deep water. Things are a struggle and the pressure is on to get things done. Maybe you might feel as if you are just treading water. What we all need is a release valve. There are so many things that people use to try and release that tension, drink, drugs, parties, and other destructive behaviours. I'm not saying that we cannot do some of these things at all; after all, there is nothing better than a good dinner party to enjoy good fellowship, and most of us need to do something different from time to time to refresh our souls, bodies, and minds. These activities do not always work for our good, though, especially if we used them as a means of escape.

So, what is the best way to pull the plug on all that stress in our lives? Let's give our burdens to God and step back and watch them disappear from the centre of our universe to the centre of His.

"Cast thy burden upon the LORD, and he shall sustain thee: he shall never suffer the righteous to be moved." Psalm 55:22.

**Challenge:** Remember to take our problems to Jesus instead of trying to escape them.

26

I was gardening one day and had to clean a garden bed to make it presentable. Cleaning a garden is a process of pulling weeds and removing dead plants in order to put in new plants. Removing weeds also means that water is not being used up by those plants that have no place there.

While I was doing this, I thought about us and how weeds are very similar to the sins in our lives. So as Jesus cleans us out, He fills the empty places with His spirit. It is the same in my garden, if the bare patches created by the removal of weeds and dead plants are not filled with new plants, it won't be long and I will find more weeds in there. This doesn't mean that we will be weed-free, but we will be more efficient for God, and bring beauty to those around us.

"And the disciples were filled with joy, and with the Holy Ghost." Acts 13:52.

Prayer: Lord, I thank you for the process of cleaning me out that goes on for the entire time of my life here on earth.

 27

Today I woke early and checked the sky; after all, I wanted to know what sort of clouds were out there. I had a load of washing to do and get dry and I would need most of the day to achieve that if it was cloudy. After breakfast I took a load of washing to the clothesline and again checked the sky, it was clear blue and there was a nice light breeze stirring the leaves on nearby trees.

The washing dried and, as I looked at the sky again later that evening, I could see through the window that a light covering of clouds had returned.

What was the message for me on this wonderful, successful washing day? God seemed to be reminding me that the clouds in life will come and go, but they will never be a permanent fixture.

I remembered my mother telling me when I was younger that the most common phrase in the Bible was "And it came to pass". As a youngster, I had wondered what that quaint phrase really meant, as I grew up, I realized that it meant what it said, that both good and bad things will come and then they will be over. Nothing in this world will last forever.

"While we look not at the things which are seen, but at the things which are not seen: for the things which are seen *are* temporal; but the things which are not seen *are* eternal." 2 Corinthians 4:18.

Challenge: Take comfort that it is only the word of God that will last forever.

28

My son wears a chainmail glove at work. It's a mesh that protects his hand while he uses knives to cut up meat. He is not allowed to start work without it. It would be too dangerous for him not to use it

When we start looking at the spiritual dangers in our world then we have only one way to protect ourselves and that is in the arms of Jesus.

"The eternal God *is thy* refuge, and underneath *are* the everlasting arms: and he shall thrust out the enemy from before thee; and shall say, Destroy *them*." Deuteronomy 33:27

Challenge: Are you seeking protection in the arms of Jesus.

29

Staying calm in amongst the busyness of life is often difficult, particularly when we have unexpected drama. When these unexpected things happen, we often declare that life has thrown a spanner in the works and they can test our patience, faith, and mental health. Of course, spanners come in very different sizes. So do life's dramas.

Faith is strengthened by exercise and often it takes a number of different spanners to tighten up the strings that attach us to our Lord and saviour, this teaches us that God will always be there to assist us in the dramas of life.

"As ye have therefore received Christ Jesus the Lord, *so* walk ye in him: Rooted and built up in him, and stablished in the faith, as ye have been taught, abounding therein with thanksgiving." Colossians 2:6-7.

Prayer: This life will throw spanners at me I know, but please help me to remember that you are faithful and therefore I can continue to trust you.

 30

I sat in the doctor's office and he looked at me and frowned, I had been right, I had another infection.

Just like the tablets that the doctor ordered for me, to work on the unseen bugs inside, God will work on my unseen sins (unseen to the outside world) and both things will improve my wellbeing, one physically, the other spiritually. I know which one will work the fastest, though.

"For all things *are* for your sakes, so that the grace which is spreading to more and more people may cause the giving of thanks to abound to the glory of God. Therefore, we do not lose heart, but though our outer man is decaying, yet our inner man is being renewed day by day." 2 Corinthians 4:15-17.

Prayer: Lord, thank you for loving me enough to keep working on me.

31

Just like the return of Jesus, no one has any idea when their time will be up. Even for those of us that get some warning due to illness, we still have no idea of the exact day or hour.

"But of that day and *that* hour knoweth no man, no, not the angels which are in heaven, neither the Son, but the Father." Mark 13:32.

Of course, once we die or Jesus returns our eternal life begins either in Heaven or Hell and there is no turning back. While it is not a good idea to dwell on death all the time, it is important to make sure that we are prepared for that final journey.

"And as it is appointed unto men once to die, but after this the judgment:" Hebrews 9:27

Prayer: Thank you, Jesus, for your gift of love that caused you to go to the cross so that we could be presented faultless before God on judgement day.

 32

On a recent trip to visit family, we spent a couple of nights close to the ocean. As I laid down waiting for sleep to take over, I listened to the noises around me. Each new place has a different sound. One particular noise dominated the night and it took me a while to register that the noise was actually the waves crashing onto the beach. Once I realized what it was, I listened with a different attitude and decided that it was God's lullaby to help me get to sleep.

Of course, during our visit, we went for a walk along the beach. On this particular stretch of beach, there was a reef of rocks, which I realized, helped make the lullaby that I had been listening to during the nights there! What I saw was the power of God at work. The sea stretched as far as the eye could see and only a God as big as the God of creation could do such an amazing thing.

And just think, He did so by saying eighteen words:

"And God said, Let the waters under the heaven be gathered together unto one place, and let the dry *land* appear: and it was so." Genesis 1:9.

Challenge: Look at the world and see God's amazing work.

33

My fingernails are on the outside, but they give me a good indication of how healthy I am on the inside. When they are strong, I can usually say that I am in good health, when they chip, crack and break then there is usually something going on that is not quite right.

I put up with bad nails for years, thinking that it was just the way things were. It wasn't until I got really healthy and my nails showed a great improvement that I realized that what I had thought was normal, actually wasn't.

This got me thinking about what our spiritual indicators of good health are. What is it that fails to be strong when we get tired, lazy, or just spiritually ill? Do our relationships with our family and friends suffer? Do we find that we are struggling to talk to our Lord on a daily basis?

Another important question is, how do we fix it? We come back to the Lord and ask Him to forgive us for letting other things get in the way of our relationship.

"Therefore also now, saith the LORD, turn ye *even* to me with all your heart, and with fasting, and with weeping, and with mourning: And rend your heart, and not your garments, and turn unto the LORD your God: for he *is* gracious and merciful, slow to anger, and of great kindness, and repenteth him of the evil." Joel 2:12-13

<u>Prayer:</u> Lord, we thank you that when we walk away from you at any time, you are just one step away, and we can return to your waiting arms instantly.

🍷 34

Many women throughout history, have had to push into areas of endeavours that they had previously been considered locked out of.

In the past, many jobs were considered to be inappropriate for women to carry out. Personally, I take my hat off to any woman who worked under the social and physical conditions that existed. I am so very grateful to the women who have worked so hard to improve these circumstances for us. These Pioneers have often had to push very hard against some of those doors that appeared to be closed. Even today many women have had to continue to march forward into career areas that are still considered more suitable to the male domain.

"That which hath been is now, and that which is to be hath already been; and God requireth that which is past." Ecclesiastes 3:15

Prayer: Thank you for the courage that you gave to those who have gone before us.

35

In Australia, we are enjoying summer, while friends in the northern hemisphere have winter. I know that on the other side of the earth, all is resting; plants and animals are hibernating, waiting for spring to come.

I guess God knows us well enough, to know that we would not rest unless we are forced to. This would be why He designed winter's short days, forcing us inside much earlier than during the long days of summer. Personally, I find winter a nice time of the year. I love being curled up in front of the heater with a good book, or writing more stories.

"While the earth remaineth, seedtime and harvest, and cold and heat, and summer and winter, and day and night shall not cease." Genesis 8:22.

Prayer: Thank you for winter when all of nature can rest up ready for the hard work of summer.

36

At a conference I attended, I noticed that the facility had a mix of classical and modern designs in the buildings. As I looked around at the people attending I also noticed that there was also a mix of old and young. As

I thought about how we present the gospel, I know that we can use a mixture of old and new technologies, however, no matter how much we desire the past or the present, there is one thing that hasn't changed down through history. That is that God inspired all the men and women who loved Him and worked for Him no matter what they did and He does not change no matter how old or new we are.

"Jesus Christ the same yesterday, and today, and forever." Hebrews 13:8.

Prayer: Lord, I thank you that your word is just as powerful today as it has been in the past.

37

As I looked around the room, I noticed some flowers I had sitting on top of our bookshelf. They were pretty and looked just like the real ones, but they didn't smell of the wonderful perfume that real ones had, because they were FAKE.

Some people come across as being real and others seem to have life so good that you have to wonder if they are lying and therefore fake. The Bible also tells us that we can be fake Christians.

"Wherefore the Lord said, Forasmuch, as this people draw near me with their mouth, and with their lips, do honour me, but have removed their heart far from me, and their fear toward me is taught by the precept of men:" Isaiah 29:13.

Challenge: May we always be real and not fake when it comes to our worship of our Lord.

38

When people take the time to sit and listen to you and you to them, good times are often the result. We are social beings, God made us that way. My reasoning is that this is one of the factors as to why we are seeing an increase in depression and anger in our society. Talking to a person, face to face, is the best medicine for many illnesses. If you enjoy yourself, you will be able to smile and laugh and that helps us. Even letting tears fall can be helpful.

"Not forsaking the assembling of ourselves together, as the manner of some *is*; but exhorting *one another*: and so much the more, as ye see the day approaching." Hebrews 10:25.

Prayer: Dear Lord, today as friends visit, please help us to build good memories that we will be able to look back on over the next few weeks.

39

We have a book that was given to my son when he was a baby. It's called "Two hands for helping". On the back cover of this little book, there is a chorus which finishes with: "Two little hands to do His will and one little heart to love him still". This is what the hands that God gave us are for. They cannot do His will without our heart loving Him. Without this love what we do with our hands will be useless.

"And though I bestow all my goods to feed *the poor*, and though I give my body to be burned, and have not charity, it profiteth me nothing." 1 Corinthians 13:3

Challenge: There are a lot of things that our hands do that God needs our hands for. So, let us work hard and with love, for Him and for mankind.

40

Most summer nights I hear the noise from the wings of mosquitoes, they come so close to my face that I can feel the air moving against my skin. These small creatures can make life very uncomfortable for so many of us, particularly after they have bitten us, leaving itchy lumps on the body.

As I am irritated by these creatures they remind me of the sins in my life, they are annoying, making my life uncomfortable and they need to be got rid of. There is only one way to deal with sin and that is to come to God and confess our sins and ask for forgiveness.

"If we confess our sins, he is faithful and just to forgive us our sins, and to cleanse us from all unrighteousness." 1 John 1:9

Prayer: Lord, please continue to help us get rid of those pesky things called sin, so that I will not annoy others with them.

41

Walking around in the dark during night, I often wonder how I would get on if I was to be inflicted with blindness, particularly after I have bumped into a wall, or have been unable to find the door to the bathroom. On such occasions, I send up a prayer for those who are blind, even if I don't know them.

I am very blessed to have my eyesight. There are various types of blindness. Have you heard "Love is blind" or "None so blind as those that will not see"?

Jesus was faced with spiritual blindness, people who would not listen to what He wanted to tell them. There are, of course, many days when I don't want to see what God wants me to see either, not confronting something is sometimes more comfortable.

"And this is the condemnation, that light is come into the world, and men loved darkness rather than light, because their deeds were evil. For every one that doeth evil hateth the light, neither cometh to the light, lest his deeds should be reproved." John 3:19-20.

Prayer: Lord please help me to see the light of your works in my life today.

 **42**

    I was taking my first two flights on a large airplane. On both occasions, I was seated behind the wings. When the plane was landing, I could see some of the workings inside that wing. There seemed to be a lot of mechanical gear in there. I was a very aware that if one of those bits broke, we could be in a lot of trouble. As I reflect on those journeys, I am amazed at the faith that is placed in so many hands. There is faith in the mechanics who built the plane, faith in the maintenance crews and faith in the pilots who fly these monsters of the skies.

    Yet ultimately, I had to place my faith, not in all these people but in God, He is the one that makes sure that all these people do the right things to make sure that that plane stays up in the air.

"And Jesus answering saith unto them, Have faith in God." Mark 11:22.

Prayer: I thank you for keeping us safe through the skills of many people.

 **43**

    One of the things I saw on a recent trip was a piece of artwork that had been created using, what appeared to be, a tree that had died where it stood on the street corner. Of course, I cannot vouch for that as a given fact.

Even from a distance, it was eye-catching and interesting but as a piece of artwork? I would never fit it in the house. It was just too big.

I was reminded that our God is too big to fit into any house. Many Sunday Schools teach children a song called "My God is so big" to help them to understand the magnitude of His love, power, and capabilities.

He spreads His love around the whole world and in fact the whole universe and across our entire history. John tells us that even Jesus, God in human form, was present right from the start when all things were created.

"In the beginning was the Word, and the Word was with God, and the Word was God. The same was in the beginning with God. All things were made by him; and without him was not anything made that was made."
John 1:1-3

Challenge: Remember that, unlike our artwork tree, God and His word will be here long after it has disintegrated into a pile of wood and metal chips.

44

Our Landscape changes all the time. In a drought, it looks brown and dry, in the morning it can be foggy or in winter it can be covered in thick frost. In the evening, bathed in the setting sun it has a different glow altogether. Of course, after the rain, it looks green and fresh, which is wonderful to see.

It reminds me of our own lives. They change all the time. From being young children, with our fresh innocent approach to life, growing up, bit by bit changing at different rates, depending on our age and the external influences that we encounter. Even as adults our lives change all the time. When we are healthy, we have a different influence on those around us. If we are going through a period of illness, we will often need people to help us, rather than us helping them. During our old age, we will be able to encourage people in very different ways to what we might do while we are young. Paul also talks about what happens as we change, both physically and spiritually:

"When I was a child, I spake as a child, I understood as a child, I thought as a child: but when I became a man, I put away childish things." 1 Corinthians 13:11

<u>Prayer:</u> Today, Lord, help me to never take the changes for granted but try to see beauty in everything.

🏆 45

Different types of lights have a habit of making objects look different. When my husband wants to inspect a property, he likes to do it first thing in the morning, because the afternoon sunlight always makes the grass appear greener - strange but true! There are such a variety of lights available now. They all have a different purpose in that they will shed a different type of light in a room. If I want to read or work, I need a clear bright light, if I want to have a romantic evening, I am going to use dimmed lights or candles.

I believe there are times in our lives when God uses different types of lights to show us the way. On some occasions He will use a strong clear light so that we can clearly see where we are to go and what we are supposed to do and yet other times He might use a dim light, one that makes us walk carefully, watching where we are going to put our feet down next.

It makes our lives very interesting and adds variety to our daily lives. I'm sure that if God used the same form of light for me each day, I would get bored and overconfident about what I was doing. God knows and understands that we need variety in our walk with Him.

"Thy word *is* a lamp unto my feet, and a light unto my path." Psalm 119:105.

<u>Prayer:</u> Lord, let us always walk carefully no matter what type of light we are walking in.

46

I was thinking about how, when we finish looking in the mirror and walk away, we often forget what we saw. When I enjoy the warmer Queensland weather, I realize that I have forgotten what it feels like to be cold. Memory is an interesting thing, isn't it? Something can be locked away for many years and then for some reason it can resurface to be mulled over again and again.

I often think about my mum, and the fact that she is now in Heaven, waiting for the rest of us to join her. While we are missing her, particularly at special family events, I know that she would not want to return to earth. It's not that she wouldn't want to celebrate with us, but she is having a better time where she is. Just like I forget about the blemishes on my face when I walk away from the mirror and the cold at home, my mother has forgotten the troubles of this earth in Heaven. She will not have forgotten about her family and friends. She will be praying for them as she waits for us and that is the blessing of having a Godly parent.

> **"Because the former troubles are forgotten, and because they are hid from mine eyes". Isaiah 65:16b.**

Challenge: Think, Oh, won't it be great to leave all our troubles behind when we move to our new home in Heaven.

47

There is a tree in my garden that is much loved, not only because of its beauty, but for the memories it provokes. The current one replaces one that was blown down during a windy day many years ago. It was given to me as a seedling. When I arrived home that day, I placed the pot on the edge of a garden, beside the carport, so that it could be kept watered until I was ready to replant it in the same position as the fallen tree. I took so long that when I actually tried to pick up the pot to replant it, the roots had grown out through the bottom and established itself right where I had sat it down. It had to stay there.

The friend that gave me the seedling was one of those ladies who, no matter how tough life was, was determined to carry on. I recall my friend who had the strength and determination to use the motto "use it or lose it". This tree reminds me that no matter what our circumstances are in life, we can work our way through the difficulties and create some beauty. Our circumstances in life may not be ideal, but we can grow, flourish, and flower right where God has placed us.

"But as God hath distributed to every man, as the Lord hath called every one, so let him walk. And so ordain I in all churches." 1 Corinthians 7:17.

Prayer: Lord, show me how to bring beauty to my world right where I am today.

48

Every now and again, I have to sort through the accumulation of papers and things that end up on my office desk. It's a matter of sorting through what is important to keep, what is not needed anymore but should be kept anyway, and what is just plain rubbish. It's something that I don't do very regularly, and it usually takes up most of the day when it happens.

Like my desk, our lives gather emotional and spiritual clutter which needs to be checked, sorted and removed. Of course, this isn't easy to dispose of. Working out what is rubbish isn't easy either. That is why Jesus promised to send us his spirit to help us with the process.

"Howbeit when he, the Spirit of truth, is come, he will guide you into all truth: for he shall not speak of himself; but whatsoever he shall hear, *that* shall he speak: and he will shew you things to come." John 16:13.

Prayer: God, you sent your spirit to help us to know the truth, help us to rely on you always for help.

 **49**

Water does things differently to other liquids when it freezes. It expands rather than shrinks. In the process of freezing, its power can break anything that may try to confine it too closely, such as a bottle, or a rock. It really smashes things apart as hail. Depending on the size of those hail stones the damage can be quite devastating. If it freezes while dripping it creates the most beautiful icicles. As frozen snow covers a community in a blanket of white, we see a beauty that can stagger the imagination.

We can also do things differently through the power of God. We can be beautiful and sparkling as we endeavour to live more and more like Jesus each day. Showing others how much He cares for the people that He created. Throughout history, many Christians have managed to break through the social issues that have confined people in difficult circumstances. I am thinking of William Wilberforce and his work to abolish slavery and Caroline Chisholm and her work amongst the convict women during the early days of Australia's European settlement. These people worked hard and consistently for many years to smash what were great social injustices.

"I can do all things through Christ which strengtheneth me." Philippians 4:13.

Prayer: God, please help us to make this world a better place to live in and give us all that we need to accomplish it

50

Looking out the window, I see ripe tomatoes on the bush. It occurred to me that without sunlight they would still be green or not even exist. I also remember a few years ago after a very long and difficult period of cloudy and wet weather, my husband came in one day and remarked that the sun had been hidden for so long that the grass had stopped growing.

Like those tomatoes, we also need the Son to ripen us, to bring us into the fullness of spirit, growth, and into the likeness of Jesus. Without Him and the work of the Holy Spirit, we would still be dead in our sins. This work in our lives creates those wonderful fruits of the spirit.

"But the fruit of the Spirit is love, joy, peace, longsuffering, gentleness, goodness, faith, Meekness, temperance: against such there is no law." Galatians 5:22-23.

"The LORD bless thee, and keep thee: The LORD make his face shine upon thee, and be gracious unto thee: The LORD lift up his countenance upon thee, and give thee peace." Numbers 6:24-26

Prayer: Oh, what a blessing it is to have your Son to enrich our lives.

51

I am very blessed because I live in Australia with a good house, good clean food, and plenty of clothes. I do need a banana a day, to keep my blood pressure normal. There are times when medication is the answer to such problems, but I am always keen to ask God if He has a better answer first.

I love my food a little too much and when I needed to find some self-control God allowed type two diabetes, gluten intolerance, low blood pressure, and allergies to guide me and develop the self-control that I needed. It is also something I still need to work on every day. I am aware that I still need to drop a few more kilos in order to be able to wear the clothes that I have been given a little more comfortably.

I'm not saying that God gave me these problems; they were a result of the stresses that I was living with over a long period of time. Maybe if I had relied on God more when I was younger, this story may have been written differently but I cannot change the past.

"And we know that all things work together for good to them that love God, to them who are the called according to *his* purpose." Romans 8:28.

<u>Prayer:</u> Lord, I am blessed to have access to all that I need and I know that you will continue to be faithful. Thank you!

52

Driving to town one day, I passed an area that had been burnt by fire. As I looked at it, even without a lot of rain, there was quite a thick covering of green grass over the entire area. Yet, there was still evidence of the damage that the fire had caused. Some of the trees looked dead; many of them covered with brown leaves and blackened trunks.

I knew, however, that it would not be long before new growth would appear on many of those trees that looked beyond recovery. There would also be many new trees sprouting, brought about by the dormant seeds being exposed to the heat of the fire.

There are times in our lives when we are tested by the fires of stress and pain. These are allowed by God to help bring about new growth in our emotional and spiritual lives making our faith stronger and sturdier.

"That the trial of your faith, being much more precious than of gold that perisheth, though it be tried with fire, might be found unto praise and honour and glory at the appearing of Jesus Christ:" 1 Peter 1:7.

Prayer: Lord, help us to know that each of the trials that we go through are to help up grow stronger in our faith, helping us to trust you more each day.

 53

It's raining, it's pouring even. While discussing the weather, as farmers do, with someone one morning, I made the comment that every time human beings get very confident in their abilities to the point of superiority, God seems to say, I'll prove to you who is stronger. This has happened so many times throughout history. If we put too much reliance on our own abilities and knowledge, we are, in fact, worshiping an idol.

If we look at the plagues of Egypt, they all proved that the God of the universe was greater than each of the god's of Egypt. (Exodus 7-12)

Even in my own life, as a teenager, I told God that I would never marry a farmer. Guess what my husband does!

Yes, it is raining! I wonder if those who have made idols out of their weather predictions will be confounded!

"You shall have no other gods before Me. Exodus 20:3

Challenge: Watch what God does, when man says it can't be done.

54

As I tried to sleep, the flashing of lightning kept breaking into the darkness. The storm was so far away that there was no sound of thunder, yet it was impressive in its power and beauty. The power was seen in its ability to light up the sky; its beauty was in the different colours against the clouds.

Again, I was reminded of how terrifying it would have been for those shepherds on the hillside outside Bethlehem all those years ago when angels appeared out of a clear night sky.

"And, lo, the angel of the Lord came upon them, and the glory of the Lord shone round about them: and they were sore afraid." Luke 2:9.

I can only imagine how spectacular the sky is going to be when Jesus returns.

"And then shall they see the Son of man coming in a cloud with power and great glory." Luke 21:27

Even though the window restricted my view of the entire spectacle, I am conscious that I have a very limited view of just how wonderful God's plan is, not only for me but for the whole of history.

"For now, we see through a glass, darkly; but then face to face: now I know in part; but then shall I know even as also I am known" 1 Corinthians 13:12

"When the Son of man shall come in his glory, and all the holy angels with him, then shall he sit upon the throne of his glory:" Matthew 25:31.

<u>**Prayer:**</u> Lord, we praise you that the bible doesn't lie, and one day we will all see just how amazing you are.

 55

I was asked what I missed most about not having my mother around. It had been twelve months since she went home to be with the Lord. As I thought about the question, I realized that it was the fellowship that we shared each week that I missed the most. It wasn't being able to ring her when I had a problem, or being able to have her arms around me when I visited, but that honest spiritual fellowship that we don't seem to share as a society anymore.

I have memories of many people sitting around their kitchen table and talking about the Lord and what He had done for them since the last time that they had been together. It was not the weather that was the major subject of the conversations, nor was it politics, even though I'm sure these were mentioned and discussed, the centre of their deliberations was God the Father, Jesus Christ, the Son, and the Holy Spirit.

As I looked around at my family with different eyes this week, I realized that we have two things in common; our parents, and the word of God being the centre of our lives as we were growing up. Other than that, we all seem to be very different people, but it's these two things that will always hold us together.

"So, we, *being* many, are one body in Christ, and every one members one of another." Romans 12:5.

Prayer: Lord, we thank you for the fellowship that we can share while we are here on earth, but look forward to better fellowship with you one day in Heaven.

56

My bags are almost packed! God willing, I will be going home tomorrow. I have had to assist my father as he packs his bags as well. It was something that my mother always did, and dad has found the prospect of doing it himself a little daunting.

In Bible study many years ago, we were discussing travelling to places, and our journey to Heaven. A wonderful Christian lady was telling our group how she hated packing because she never knew what to take. She told us how she would put things in and then take them out again and so the process became rather tiresome.

One member of our group turned to her and said, "Well, you won't have to worry about what you pack for Heaven, you have everything you need already." What a wonderful thought, if we have Christ in our lives, no matter what we are doing, where we are, or how it happens, we are packed and ready to go when He calls us. He is all we need, to take that final journey home.

"Jesus saith unto him, I am the way, the truth, and the life: no man cometh unto the Father, but by me." John 14:6.

Prayer: Thank you for being the way to Heaven for us, Lord Jesus.

 **57**

Time has had a very different dimension since losing my mum as a result of an accident. I am far more aware of the need to get things done and just how necessary it is for me to not let time hang heavy. If I do, then I know that I am going to slip down into that dark pit of depression. It was her time to go and it's still my time to live and God still has work for me to do here. I am glad, however, that I do not know when my time will be up. I just need to work for God until He calls me home as well.

"To everything, there is a season, and a time to every purpose under the heaven; A time to be born, and a time to die; ... A time to break down and a time to build up; A time to weep and a time to laugh; a time to mourn and a time to dance;" Ecclesiastes 3:1-4.

Prayer: Lord I know my mother lives outside of time now, but I must still live within its confines, please help me to use it wisely.

 **58**

As I think about my grandfather, and all those men who went off to war because they would not shirk their duty, I have to feel a little shame.

Many of those men, who were called up for service, didn't want to fight. They hated killing, they saw it as evil, and still, they did their duty! Yes, they marched into battle, determined to make sure that the country that they called home would be a safe place for their families and their loved ones that weren't even born yet.

There is another person who did not draw back from his duty and that was Jesus. He went to the cross because He loved us.

"For God so loved the world, that he gave his only begotten Son, that whosoever believeth in him should not perish, but have everlasting life." John 3:16.

Prayer: Thank you, Lord, for giving us such a gift of love.

 **59**

What I like about nature, is its ability to recover from the devastating events that it is put through. Our country is often subjected to horrific bushfires, winds, droughts, and floods. Even my garden is subjected to considerable periods of neglect from time to time, depending on what other issues I have to deal with, and yet, it still manages to bounce back to life once I start caring for it again.

So, what is the secret of this marvellous ability to recuperate? I can only point to the amazing God who created it in the first place. He did such a good job of creating the world, He looked at what he made at the end of each day and declared that it was good. (Genesis 1)

Another great thing is that we are also part of God's created wonders, and when we are put through the storms of life, we can call on Him to help repair any bumps and bruises.

"And Jesus answering said unto them, they that are whole need not a physician; but they that are sick." Luke 5:31

He promises that He will help us if only we ask Him in Jeremiah 33:3 He says,

"Call unto me, and I will answer thee, and shew thee great and mighty things, which thou knowest not."

Prayer: Each time I look around me and see the landscape recovering from a disaster, I can remind myself that you are the powerful God of creation, and so willing to help me through any of my tough times.

 **60**

When I read the story of creation, I see that the sun was not made until the fourth day, but He commanded on day three,

"Let the earth bring forth grass, the herb yielding seed and the fruit tree yielding fruit after his kind whose seed is in itself, upon the earth and it was so." (Genesis 1:11)

And in Revelation 21:23 we are told that

"The city had no need of the sun, neither of the moon to shine in it; for the glory of God did lighten it and the Lamb is the light thereof."

This tells me that God's light is stronger than our sunshine but, for our limited time here on earth, sunshine is a very necessary thing.

It is a well-known fact that without sunshine the grass, trees, flowers, and crops won't grow. A few years back we had a lot of rain over an extended period of time. With continuously cloudy days for a few weeks, the crops stopped growing. They needed the rain but they also needed the sunshine.

While we won't need our sunshine in Heaven, I'm very glad that we have it here on Earth and can enjoy the things it gives us; growth, shade, and patterns on my veranda as it shines through the leaves.

Prayer: Lord, I thank you for the sunshine and the way you make our world able to grow lots of good things for us to use.

61

Often the first verses that come to my mind in the morning is Lamentations 3:22-23

> **"It is of the Lord's mercies that we are not consumed, because his compassions fail not. They are new every morning: great is thy faithfulness."**

When we experience long periods of drought, it becomes a habit to get jumpy after more than a few days of dry weather. So, I'm thankful when God has been merciful and sent us more rain.

I am aware that we stereotype what we believe "mercies" are. Do we think of mercies as always being good things, such as rain? Mercies are also the dry spells in the weather and our lives.

I am reminded of the saying: "Sometimes you have to be cruel to be kind". We know that not every request our children present to us is good for them, and so it's important for us to say that dreaded word "No". We know that sometimes giving good gifts actually means withholding things from our children, that may not be bad in themselves, but inappropriate at their age and development. We have some idea of the consequences of giving things to our children too early.

Now God knows us much better, He also knows what the consequences will be, simply because He can see the future and has planned it.

> **"If ye then, being evil, know how to give good gifts unto your children: how much more shall *your* heavenly Father give the Holy Spirit to them that ask him?" Luke 11:13.**

Prayer: Lord, I thank you for those things I don't like, because I know that your mercies are things that I just cannot see yet.

 **62**

There are many days when I really don't look forward to getting old. So, what is the value of old? We bought a property that had an old house and shed on it. The advice that we were given at the time was to bulldoze the lot and start again. Yes, I agree there are times when this would be an appropriate strategy, but I fear that sometimes it's a tactic that is used way too often.

The bible tells us in Ecclesiastes 1:9 that:

"The thing that hath been, it *is that* which shall be; and that which is done *is* that which shall be done: and *there is* no new *thing* under the sun."

I realize that some people may have trouble believing this. We cannot have new technologies without them being based on older stuff.

In order to move forward, we often have to come to terms, and make peace, with our past. My experience has been that my future can be made a little better by combining the old with the new. Not everything old is "old hat" and we can learn a lot by revisiting history.

There are many people who would like to scrap outdated things and start over. But everything has a connection to the past. If we dispose of the history of a society, for instance, we lose a lot of their lessons and knowledge that could be of great value to those trying to make their way in the world a hundred or so years from now.

Prayer: Lord, help us to learn from our past but not to keep living in it.

63

God knows all about my needs and concerns, big and small. He even knows how things will be worked out. My heart, though, is having trouble keeping up. This just proves how human I am.

"And it shall come to pass, that before they call, I will answer; and while they are yet speaking, I will hear." Isaiah 65:24.

Prayer: Lord, thank you for knowing everything about me, help me to wait for you to act.

64

All our paths go in different directions. It doesn't matter who we are or where we live, life will be a journey that will be different for every one of us. Some journeys will be straight and long with very few corners, like the great straight highways in the deserts. Others will have many corners, uphill grades and downhill runs, and others will be bumpy rides. Each journey is designed by the great designer, the one that knows exactly who you are and what you will respond to best. He will lead you to a place where He has great work for you to do. Most likely, you will not see it as a great work, but it will be, because it is the job that He has planned for you, and you will affect someone in a very special way.

It doesn't matter where our journey takes us, what is important, is that when we reach the end, we will be able to say with Paul:

"I have fought a good fight, I have finished *my* course, I have kept the faith: Henceforth there is laid up for me a crown of righteousness, which the Lord, the righteous judge, shall give me at that day: and not to me only, but unto all them also that love his appearing." 2 Timothy 4:7-8

Challenge: No matter what the design is, let us all tread our paths faithfully.

🍷 65

Road signs point towards the direction you want people to go, not where they have come from. If road signs did actually point you to where you had come from, they would be the most useless things in existence. You would be a very strange person if you did not know where you had come from.

When it comes to travelling our life's journey, Paul tells us not to look back while we are trying to move forward in life.

"Brethren, I count not myself to have apprehended: but *this* one thing *I do*, forgetting those things which are behind, and reaching forth unto those things which are before," Philippians 3:13

We all need to keep our eyes on where we are going, not where we have been.

What about the pointy structures on church buildings called steeples? These too, are meant to direct people to think about heavenly things rather than earthly things. Paul encourages us to do this in Colossians 3:1-2:

"If ye then be risen with Christ, seek those things which are above, where Christ sitteth on the right hand of God. Set your affection on things above, not on things on the earth."

There are signs that actually point in the wrong direction and if we follow them we end up in the wrong place or completely lost. God however always knows where we are and can bring us home as soon as we ask.

Prayer: Lord, may I follow your signs in the right direction so I don't get lost.

66

The rainbow represents the promise by God not to destroy the world with a flood as He did in the days of Noah.

"I set my rainbow in the cloud, and it will be a sign of a covenant between me and the earth." Genesis 9:13.

You can read the whole story in Genesis 6:9-9:17.

When I look in the sky, I don't often get to see a full rainbow. More often than not I see only part of the arch across the sky. The other day I saw a very unusual, small part of a rainbow and my first thought was: Sometimes, you have to hang onto the small part of the promise that you can see, and use faith for the rest.

There are times in life when we find ourselves bombarded with so many problems that it can be very easy to feel weighed down and overcome. Yet, God has a promise for each situation and trial but in the midst of all that we are dealing with, it is hard to find any hope.

Challenge: Hang on to the smallest promise, verse or phrase and grip it with all your might and slowly you will find the rest of the answers that God has for you because the rest of the rainbow does exist.

67

I came across a waterhole one day and, swimming around on the water, was a duck. Its progress through the water seemed to be so effortless and smooth. What I couldn't see, was how hard the duck's legs were moving out of sight under the surface to make the movement seem so easy.

Even when it comes to my own life, God is working behind the scenes, unseen by me to bring His plan into action. There are many times when I will not see what God has saved me from or prevented me from doing, but He has a plan, and His plan will work out because of His love and care for me and those around me.

"Casting all your care upon him; for he careth for you." 1 Peter 5:7.

Prayer: Thank you, Lord, for caring so much for me.

 **68**

My husband left for town with a motorbike on board which had been playing up for days. My son and I were trying to right some equipment that had been blown over during a storm, when we noticed that one of the dogs had shredded his collar. I knew we didn't have a spare one in stock and my husband didn't have his mobile with him. A phone call was made to the store that he was heading to, I left a message, asking them to pass it on. I have to admit though, as I hung up, that I had my doubts that my husband would actually receive the message. I was wrong, he did and arrived home a couple of hours later with collar in hand.

This made me think about modern equipment and what was working or not working. In the storm, we had water in our taps because we have a high tank, not an electric pump. I am able to light my wood burning stove if the electricity is cut off, enabling me to cook meals for my family. My husband's motorbike is not working, but his legs do. Our old-fashioned fridge works, while a mate of my son's new one has stopped working, even while it was under warranty.

So, my simple pleasure is in the old fashioned things that work, such as old fashioned service that passes on messages, and equipment that isn't complicated to use.

Some people think that trusting in God is old fashioned, but one thing I know, is that He is very reliable and will work things for my good.

"Trust in him at all times; ye people, pour out your heart before him: God *is* a refuge for us. Selah." Psalm 62:8.

Prayer: Lord, help me to trust you to allow you to work in my life and do what you ask without complaint.

🏆 69

Oh, there are so many beautiful things in this world, and what one person thinks is beautiful doesn't always appeal to someone else. We picked up a piece of pottery at an auction sale once, it is the ugliest thing I've ever seen, but I'm sure that someone, including its creator, thinks it is wonderfully beautiful.

As I have struggled with pain, I have complained to God about how I wish this whole situation was over. He, in turn, has reminded me of a story of a man who, having worked in a leprosy facility, found himself unable to feel pain. Of course, the question was, did he have leprosy, or some other virus? Only time would tell. So, about six weeks later he was preparing his vegetables for dinner when he hurt himself, he felt pain, and it was beautiful. Why? Simply because, when he was able to feel the pain, he knew that he didn't have leprosy.

Feeling pain tells us that something is wrong. That something is happening that is not normal. There are many different sorts of pain and not everyone feels the same way when experiencing it. When it comes to the pain of loneliness, depression, or anger, we all react differently, but:

"Who comforteth us in all our tribulation, that we may be able to comfort them which are in any trouble, by the comfort wherewith we ourselves are comforted of God." 2 Corinthians 1:4.

Prayer: Lord, thank you for pain.

🍷 70

A logo lets people know instantly which company the product you are looking at comes from. It is usually different and distinctive to each particular company.

Some organisations or groups of people can be identified in other ways, their uniforms, style of clothes or the vehicles they drive. I remember one day, years ago, going with my daughter to collect some animals for a special "Animal Farm Day". As we pulled up at the gate a lady walked out of the house dressed in a specific manner. My daughter and I looked at each other and went "oh wow". The way this lady was dressed identified her as being a member of a charity group. They all dressed in the same way. I can remember thinking shouldn't Christians stand out like this lady did.

We are meant to stand out. Our behaviour towards our fellow man, our love towards the unlovely, our enemies and sinners; this is supposed to be our logo. Do we wear our logo through our actions or hide it by blending in.

"By this shall all *men* know that ye are my disciples, if ye have love one to another." John 13:35.

Prayer: Lord, may I behave in a manner that helps you to stand out.

🍷 71

What would our lives look like if they didn't have any colour? This is of course not the way God has made our world. He has filled it with a rainbow of hues, colours of every variety, depth, and tone. Each colour has a different effect on our emotions, which in turn affects our moods.

"And out of the ground made the LORD God to grow every tree that is pleasant to the sight, and good for food;" (Genesis 2:9a)

There is also another colour in our lives, the ups, and downs of life. How boring would our lives be if we didn't experience sadness, happiness, love, hate, joy, peace, stress, quietness, and storms of existence? These things colour our lives not only by providing variety, but they also give us opportunities to learn, grow, gain strength, find our weaknesses, and just connect with others. Life will consist of the good, the bad and the ugly.

We only have to turn the news on to see that is the case. When we feel the pain, we are reassured that we are alive and it helps us to learn how to make sensible decisions, even though it is through painful circumstances. Variety is the spice of life and therefore the colour of our world.

"I call heaven and earth to record this day against you, *that* I have set before you life and death, blessing and cursing: therefore, choose life, that both thou and thy seed may live:" Deuteronomy 30:19.

Prayer: Lord, thank you for the variety of the colours that you have given us.

72

Today as I type my stories, I have my internet modem charging on my left. It needs to be charged from time to time or it fails to work. If it doesn't work, then the side effects are, that I cannot use my computer to its greatest capacity.

We all need to recharge from time to time. Usually, it happens while we sleep. God gave us the night for a reason. It was so we could sleep, let our bodies rest and assist in whatever healing needs to happen from the day to day wear and tear on our bodies.

Spiritual recharging also needs to happen on a regular basis and I mean more than once a week on Sundays. I thank the Lord for the internet as I am able to recharge as I read other Christians work, thoughts, and posts. It also helps me with my research. Yes, I'm probably a little lazier these days, but I love being able to give Mr. Google a few keywords and have a number of options given back to me. I just don't have the photographic memory that my mother had.

"My presence will go with you, and I will give you rest." Exodus 33:14.

Challenge: Do something to recharge your spiritual life today.

 **73**

There are a lot of things that seem to automatically go together. Things like salt and pepper, music and song, joy and laughter or life and death. There seems to be difficulty separating the two when we think about one, the other comes to mind.

Some of these things are similar while others are complete opposites. After all music and song are similar but life and death are opposites but life is full of those sorts of mysteries. There are times when different people can work together to achieve all sorts of outcomes and help each other in diverse ways.

"But we all, with open face beholding as in a glass the glory of the Lord, are changed into the same image from glory to glory, *even* as by the Spirit of the Lord." 2 Corinthians 3:18.

Prayer: I pray that no matter how long I live that I will allow Jesus to work in my life to create in me an improvement of my personality and make me more like Him.

74

It amazes me that it doesn't seem to matter what time I wake up, even if it is in the middle of the night, I can hear the birds singing. It seems to me that they always find something to be happy about. It doesn't matter how hot the weather is they still find the energy to sing. I have to admit though that just after it rains, they seem to sing just a little more chirpily. While I can hear these wonderful creatures and their songs on a daily basis, seeing them is very difficult

It reminds me in some small way about trying to see God. We can see the evidence of His creation, but we cannot see God Himself. The proof is in the rain that falls, the trees that grow, the flowers that come out in such a wide variety of colours, the blue sky, the green grass, and the birds themselves. These things are wonderful and give us something to be happy about on their own.

"But ask now the beasts, and they shall teach thee; and the fowls of the air, and they shall tell thee: Or speak to the earth, and let it teach you; and let the fish of the sea declare to you. Who among all these does not know That the hand of the LORD has done this,..." Job 12:7-9.

<u>**Prayer:**</u> All we have to do is study the wonders of nature to learn about how wonderful and gracious you are God.

75

When I was at school, we were given exercises such as two pictures that were almost the same and we had to find ten or so things that were different. Why were such challenges presented to us? I think they were supposed to help us observe and find the subtle differences in the pictures; training our brains to look carefully, focus, and maybe assist us in picking up on something that was slightly out of place, or not quite right in real life. Successful? I really have no idea.

We are warned in the bible to check all that we are told because it is so easy for others to twist what God says and make it mean something different. The first incident of this was when the serpent talked to Eve in the garden and as a result, sin entered our world. The problem has been an issue ever since.

He understood how easy it is for people to be confused by what others say. So, he is putting the responsibility back on us to make sure that what we are being told is true and correct. The best way to do this is to pray and read God's word for ourselves every day.

"Beloved, believe not every spirit, but try the spirits whether they are of God: because many false prophets are gone out into the world." 1 John 4:1

<u>**Prayer:**</u> Lord, help us spot the subtle differences that make things not quite right.

 **76**

Once when I was traveling home from Sydney, I was thinking about the statement of signed, sealed, and delivered. We travelled by train for most of the day and then on a bus for the last 3 hours, I realized that the bus is signed, the roads are sealed and I was delivered home safe and sound.

If I want to relate this to my life's journey, there was a time when Jesus signed my name into the book of life.

"Notwithstanding in this rejoice not, that the spirits are subject unto you; but rather rejoice, because your names are written in heaven." Luke 10:20

He sealed my salvation with His blood on the cross.

"In whom ye also *trusted*, after that ye heard the word of truth, the gospel of your salvation: in whom also after that ye believed, ye were sealed with that holy Spirit of promise," Ephesians 1:13

And one day I will be delivered home to Heaven

"And to wait for his Son from heaven, whom he raised from the dead, *even* Jesus, which delivered us from the wrath to come." 1 Thessalonians 1:10

Prayer: Lord, I can be grateful for all the times that the trains and buses keep me safe all the way from where I have been and home again.

 **77**

I was thinking about words we use that have two meanings. The first one that came to mind is the word "fear". We are told in Joshua 1:9:

"Have not I commanded thee? Be strong and of a good courage; be not afraid, neither be thou dismayed: for the LORD thy God *is* with thee whithersoever thou goest."

And yet in Proverbs 9:10 we are told:

"The fear of the LORD *is* the beginning of wisdom: and the knowledge of the holy *is* understanding."

In the first verse, we are told not to be scared of what is happening around us. Some people have been told to be afraid of a judgemental God. If we do something wrong, He will strike us with lightning but this is not the sort of God we have. We have a loving God, but a God who is also just and fair. While we are here on earth, He will reach out to us and forgive us when we ask it of Him.

"For I will be merciful to their unrighteousness, and their sins and their iniquities will I remember no more." Hebrews 8:12.

The other verse, Proverbs 9:10, refers to us being so amazed at what God can do, that we just stand there and watch His wonderful plan unfold. I am sure that sometimes you just cannot help but be staggered by what our God does.

Challenge: Are you amazed by what God does?

 **78**

Red is for Love, Beauty, Courage and Respect, Oh Wow! Can anyone guess what I am thinking? Matthew 26:28 says: "For this is my blood of the new testament, which is shed for many for the remission of sins." What love and courage was expressed by His sacrifice? That enables us to share in the beauty of life and when we committed our lives to Jesus, we are showing that we respect, just how much it cost our God to allow Jesus to go to the cross.

I would assume that this is why, it has been the tradition to present someone with a red rose when we would like to express our love for them.

"For God so loved the world, that he gave his only begotten Son, that whosoever believeth in him should not perish, but have everlasting life." John 3:16.

Another thing that red often represents is anger, when we say, "I saw red", we are not saying we loved what we saw, we are saying that what we saw or heard made us angry.

It can also be used to warn us of danger.

How strange that the same colour can have so many different meanings. We can choose how we react to any given situation.

Challenge: Let us make a choice to love, not to react with anger or fear.

79

In my garden, I have a Dahlia Tree. It is positioned in a protected corner behind the shed. They seem to flower very late in the season just about the time the frosts start to cover the ground some mornings. The plant grows high enough so the flowers can be seen only by looking up into the sky and so highlight frosts don't kill the flower. It could be said that the flowers are up in the air.

As I enjoy the beauty of the flowers, I am reminded that my mother used to say that some Christians are so angelic, always up in the air harping, that they were of no earthly use. I know that high ideals and looking up are good things. It is also important that, when it comes to relating to those people on the ground who are coping with the frosts of life, I need to be real and down to earth.

In Matthew 25:31-46, we read about how on judgment day God will separate the sheep from the goats. The sheep represent those people who have helped their fellow citizens by giving them food, clothes, and shelter, very ordinary and necessary things for everyone to survive. These are the "down to earth" things that we are to do to help those who have found themselves out in the cold.

"And the King shall answer and say unto them, Verily I say unto you, inasmuch as ye have done *it* unto one of the least of these my brethren, ye have done *it* unto me." Matthew 25:40.

Prayer: Thank you, Lord, for making us unique individuals with diverse talents. Please show us each day how to do some earthly good.

80

Getting a perspective on something is always easier with hindsight. Wouldn't it be wonderful if we could have foresight as good as hindsight? It's not about the ability to know what is going to happen but that ability to understand the consequences of the decisions that we make today. One of the things that I have loved to be able to do as a kid was to understand what people were trying to do when they would ask me questions.

As the distance grows between us and the events in our past, we learn so much about what happened and how to handle a situation if it comes up again.

God does not have to look back, He can see everything from beginning to end and therefore knows how everything is going to work out. This is not only because of His perspective but because He made the plan in the first place.

"Declaring the end from the beginning, And from ancient times things which have not been done, Saying, 'My purpose will be established, And I will accomplish all My good pleasure';" Isaiah 46:10 (NAS)

Prayer: Lord, I thank you that you have a plan, not only for me but for every person that has ever lived and all of history.

🍷 81

As I age, I need to keep writing myself a note to remind me of what I have to do. In fact, I have to write myself lots of notes. Old age and a good short-term memory do not seem to go hand in hand.

I guess God understood that our memories are always going to be a problem. That is why we are told so many times in the Bible to talk and write about all the good things that God does for us. This is to keep us focused on the blessings that He showers us with on daily basis. It is also important for us to use our memories to teach our children about the faithfulness of God.

"And thou shalt teach them diligently unto thy children, and shalt talk of them when thou sittest in thine house, and when thou walkest by the

way, and when thou liest down, and when thou risest up." Deuteronomy 6:7.

Challenge: *Write a list of blessings that you have received today and thank God for each one of them.*

82

Among the many passions that I have, I would list writing and applying the word of God to what I write as my most recent. This is a relatively new passion for me but I have always attacked everything I did with great passion giving more than 100 percent effort. It seems to me that if God loves me enough to allow His son to die on the cross, then it seems a very small thing for me to return His love by doing the very best that I can at what I do for Him.

"Whatsoever thy hand findeth to do, do *it* with thy might; for *there is* no work, nor device, nor knowledge, nor wisdom, in the grave, whither thou goest." Ecclesiastes 9:10

"And whatsoever ye do, do *it* heartily, as to the Lord, and not unto men;" Colossians 3:23

Prayer: Lord, help me to give 100% to everything I do.

83

I have two names. Helen is the one that most people know me by now and another one is the one my father gave me. My father knew that every child needs someone to look up to and, as he loved the wonderful qualities of my mother, he gave me her first name. If I had been named for my personality, I should have been called Norma, but of course, when I was named, my personality was hidden from my parents. Names are such tricky things. We are seeing a great variety of names that parents are giving to their children, particularly celebrities.

So why did I change my name? As I have always stated, I have a lot of my father's DNA in me. As a young person, trying to be the same as my mother was such a struggle that depression was always snapping at my heels. So, one-night, God and I had a very long conversation about my middle name as the name to be known by. This way I live my life as who He had made me not who I wanted to be.

Some people even suggested that St Peter wouldn't recognize me when I got to the gates of Heaven. God changed peoples' names in the Bible plenty of times. Abram to Abraham, Sara to Sarah, Saul to Paul, Simon to Peter. So, I don't think there will be any problems when I get to the Pearly Gates.

"Can a woman forget her sucking child, that she should not have compassion on the son of her womb? yea, they may forget, yet will I not forget thee." Isaiah 49:15.

<u>Prayer:</u> Lord, I thank you that you will not forget who I really am.

🍷 84

In my garden I have a statue of a lady hiding her head in her arms, looking a little despaired. As I looked at it one morning, I thought about how occasionally people have posted that their angels might think about them in this manner, that we get into trouble so many times that they despair of us ever being able to get things right.

My musings were interrupted by this thought: "If God didn't love me so unconditionally, He might feel that way about me as well". So, isn't it wonderful that He does love us all so unconditionally?

"For God so loved the world, that he gave his only Son, that whoever believes in him should not perish but have eternal life." John 3:16 (ESV)

Prayer: Thank you, Father, for your unconditional love.

 **85**

My suitcase holds all the clothes that I will be wearing when I am away from home. It reminds me of the temporary status that we have here on this earth. We will not always be here and while we are here, we should travel light.

What do I mean by traveling light? Let us not carry around burdens that are not ours, let us shed the burdens of anger, malice, and spite, for these are very heavy weights to carry? Let us instead pack our bags with forgiveness, peace, calmness, and contentment, for these are very light things to carry and can have a great impact on those we meet during our life's journey.

Etienne de Grellet said: "I shall pass this way but once; any good that I can do or any kindness I can show to any human being; let me do it now. Let me not defer nor neglect it, for I shall not pass this way again."

"Whereas ye know not what *shall be* on the morrow. For what *is* your life? It is even a vapour, that appeareth for a little time, and then vanisheth away. For that ye *ought* to say, If the Lord will, we shall live, and do this, or that." James 4:14-15

Challenge: May we look around us and find something nice to say or do each day.

🍷 86

One morning I woke to a thick foggy cloud covering our driveway. It is true that we live in a foggy world, one that is hard to see where we are going clearly. At each turn, we are bombarded with information and advice. We then have to sort through all that material to work out what is true, suitable and right for our particular situation.

As I looked at what I could see of our driveway, I thought about how carefully I would need to drive when I got my vehicle out. I realized that there would be many people who would get behind the wheel of their car and drive madly headlong into the fog while others would slow down and take as much care as they could.

Isn't that also true of people in this world? Some people charge headlong into life. They drive themselves, work hard and climb madly to the top of the business world. They often do not care who they hurt along the way. There are other people who also make their way in the world with careful consideration not only for how they can help other people but also about what God would like them to achieve.

"If it be possible, as much as lieth in you, live peaceably with all men. Dearly beloved, avenge not yourselves, but *rather* give place unto wrath: for it is written, Vengeance *is* mine; I will repay, saith the Lord. Therefore, if thine enemy hunger, feed him; if he thirsts, give him drink: for in so doing thou shalt heap coals of fire on his head. Be not overcome of evil, but overcome evil with good." Romans 12:18-21

Prayer: Lord, help us to drive carefully through life.

🍷 87

We listen to the weather report every night. We often wake up in the mornings to find that the clouds were lying very heavily on the ground despite the last night's broadcast of clear sky and sunshine. I keep thinking about the unreliability of the weather bureau. They just don't seem to have a clue about the weather and what it will do.

It has occurred to me that we have put far too much faith in these weather predictions. Just because the pictures from space tell us that the clouds are coming and the computer models tell us that we are going to get a certain amount of rain from the same cloud formations, does not make it right. Why? Because the satellites and computers do not control the clouds or the rain. God does!

When it comes to weather prediction I often think of the passage in the Bible where mankind had decided that they could build a tower that would reach to the heavens.

Genesis 11:1-10 tells the full story and verse 7 says:

"Come, let's go down, and there confuse their language, that they may not understand one another's speech."

This is how God put a stop to their pride. I sometimes think that is what God does with the weather. When humans are so sure that they know what is going to happen, He deals with our pride in a variety of ways.

Challenge: To remember that God will have the final say about everything that happens in this world.

88

Researching the meaning of Yellow I found the colour yellow stands for freshness, happiness, positivity, clarity, energy, optimism, enlightenment, remembrance, intellect, honour, loyalty, and joy, but on the other, it represents cowardice and deceit. I noticed that there was a picture of bananas beside this definition which is probably appropriate as I need to eat a banana a day to keep my blood pressure at a level that stops me from getting dizzy. Bananas are also classed as a high energy food along with being a good source of potassium, something we all need.

Again, there is another side, that dark side to this colour; cowardice and deceit. There always is that flip side to everything here on earth. I guess it's no accident that the sun that wakes us up in the mornings is also yellow in colour, or that the flames of a fire that help keep us warm and happy in winter are also yellow.

Maybe that is why the streets of Heaven are paved with Gold; to give us a constant feeling of happiness, not that we will need it.

"The twelve gates *were* twelve pearls: each individual gate was of one pearl. And the street of the city *was* pure gold, like transparent glass."
Revelation 21.21

Challenge: Are we asking God to help us see the good things instead of the bad things?

89

Tea, it has to be said, is my favourite drink. It was one of the few things that I could continue drink after I was diagnosed as a diabetic. I prefer to drink my tea in a mug rather than a cup because mugs seem to hold more tea. I have a variety of mugs in my cupboard. One that was bought for me by one of my children says: "Now Panic and Freak Out". I'm often accused of doing this but I would argue against it. Yes, I have been known to raise my voice but, like many people say, it is to me a form of motivational speaking to my children. How else will they understand the urgency of a situation unless my tone changes? I'm not saying that I have never sinned in this process.

The mug does serve as a reverse psychology prompt, though. It reminds me that it is really a very silly thing to do and a great waste of time. It is a very interesting way of reminding me that God is control of my life. He has a plan for it and He has an answer for any problem that I could be confronted with.

> **"For I know the thoughts that I think toward you, saith the LORD, thoughts of peace, and not of evil, to give you an expected end."**
> **Jeremiah 29:11.**

<u>**Prayer:**</u> Thank you, Lord, for the plan that you have for my life.

 **90**

I have to admit that the most common daily ritual that I carry out is checking my Facebook messages and notifications. My reason is that we live at least twenty minutes from town and all our neighbours are busy people. It seems that I cannot match the time I have available to their available time. So, Facebook becomes my social connection to the outside world.

God made us social creatures and we need to talk to people in the good and bad times. There was a reason why God created Eve for Adam and there is a reason why He tells us not to forget to meet with other Christians.

> **"Not forsaking the assembling of ourselves together, as the manner of some *is*; but exhorting *one another*: and so much the more, as ye see the day approaching." Hebrews 10:25.**

Having had to deal with depression for most of my life, I understand the need to socialise. As I listen to people who tell us that we need to attend counselling to combat the "black dog" as it's called here in Australia, I silently think that if we talked to our neighbours, friends and those in the street more often we would find that many of the mild cases would just evaporate. I know that if I'm having a bad day there is usually someone on Facebook who has something encouraging to say, brightening my day.

Prayer: Lord, please help me to make sure that I have something encouraging to say that helps someone get through their day.

 91

My favourite pastime at present is writing short stories. I'm not very good at it and I am always amazed when people tell me that I am talented. When I was at school, I had trouble with reading, spelling, and arithmetic. My break came when I reached thirty-something, it was discovered that I had an eye co-ordination problem. It turned out that my eyes were not working together in the way they should have been.

So, my desire to write seemed like an impossible dream, well, that was until God allowed someone to invent the computer and more importantly 'spell checker'. I still use that facility a lot. Without this technology, I would never be able to write a short story, let alone three hundred and sixty-five. There are still days when my lack of skills really gets me down, and I feel as if I am truly out of my depth.

On these occasions, I have to remind myself that God has helped me to do this. What His reasons are, I have no idea, but I will keep going for the moment and I praise Him each time someone is encouraged by something that I present.

There are two verses that keep coming to mind during those bad moments that I have and they are:

"I can do all things through Christ which strengtheneth me." Philippians 4:13 and

"For my thoughts *are* not your thoughts, neither *are* your ways my ways, saith the LORD." Isaiah 55:8.

Prayer: Lord, I thank you for the talents and technology that help me to spread your word.

92

When we use the phrase, "the heart of the matter", we are referring to the core and the basic centre of something. This is because we have always understood that the heart, as an organ, is in the centre of the chest and without it, we do not live. Not here on earth anyway!

This is a great thought when you think that God is the centre of the universe and without Him, we would not have a life. The universe would not exist.

"In the beginning, God created the heaven and the earth and the earth was without form, and void; and darkness *was* upon the face of the deep. And the Spirit of God moved upon the face of the waters." Genesis 1:1-2.

"In the beginning was the Word, and the Word was with God, and the Word was God. The same was in the beginning with God. All things were made by him, and without him was not anything made that was made."
John 1:1-3

Prayer: Lord, thank you for being the centre and life of the universe and that, without you, we would not have a life at all.

93

When it comes to "having a heart", we refer to the way people care. So it is that, the more people care, the bigger their heart is. We say that caring people have a good heart. Hearts are associated with love; love leads to caring; love and caring will often lead us to do extraordinary things for others, often strangers. Who did the most extraordinary thing for mankind, not strangers but His own creation? A creation that was formed out of extraordinary love.

"For God so loved the world, that he gave his only begotten Son, that whosoever believeth in him should not perish, but have everlasting life."
John 3:16

Prayer: Jesus, my Lord and Saviour, I thank you for your extraordinary act of love towards me and mankind.

🍷 94

It's the end of the day; there have been the usual things that need to be attended to. Maybe there have been dramas and maybe it's just been an ordinary day. Each night when I can finally call it "day over", I climb in between the sheets and relax. I might watch a TV show, read a book, or check my Facebook for a while, but the last thing I do before going to sleep, is talk to God.

Like David in Psalm 4, I tell Him about the things that are bothering me, those sins that I know I have committed and the things that I think might be a problem for my friends. Things that have made me happy, worries I have about our children and the things that I not only would like to do the next day but in the weeks, months and years ahead of me. I know that my God hears me because over my lifetime He has proven to me that He does hear me and has answered so many of the prayers that I have offered up to Him particularly when I have asked Him to take away the anger in my heart. After I finish talking, I know that I can lie down in peace and sleep.

"Casting all your care upon him; for he careth for you." 1 Peter 5:7.

Prayer: Lord, I have no idea about what the next day may bring but I know that you will always be there for me, to help me, motivate, inspire, and push me forward.

95

According to Wikipedia: "A *hobby* is a regular activity that is done for pleasure, typically during one's leisure time. Hobbies can include collecting themed items and objects, engaging in creative and artistic pursuits, playing sports, or pursuing other amusements."

So, according to this definition, my hobby is writing. I mostly use a computer to carry out this hobby but over the last couple of days, I have been reminded that the old-fashioned pen and paper has its place.

My mother starting sending her sister cards instead of making regular phone calls when her sister's hearing and memory was starting to deteriorate. The cards could be read over and over again but a phone call would be forgotten almost as soon as the call ended. The card was one way for her sister to know that she wasn't forgotten and she was loved.

For those without modern technology available, the old fashion methods still have great value. It's not about keeping an old tradition alive but about being relevant to those who don't have the same advantages as I do.

"And as ye would that men should do to you, do ye also to them likewise." Luke 6:31.

Prayer: Lord, help us to remember that sometimes doing things the old-fashioned way has its value and that you can work through these things still.

96

When people say that something is homemade, they usually mean that they made it themselves. But did they? I looked up the word 'made' to see how many times it appears in the bible. The result was one thousand three hundred and twenty-one times. There are eleven mentions of the word in the first two chapters of the book of Genesis. What does this mean to me in relation to homemade? It means that without the hand of God making me and the raw materials to start with, I would not be able to make anything. In fact, what I call "homemade" isn't really homemade at all, it is some things God has already made rearranged to give me something else.

God even made my imagination that writes poems and stories and puts my cards together. He created those whose imaginations have managed to; invent such things as the steam engine, harness electricity, work out how to make computers more efficient, solve medical issues, and build the great structures that our city skylines are known for. Yet, so many times I fear that I do not give credit to God enough for these things.

"He hath made every*thing* beautiful in his time: also, he hath set the world in their heart, so that no man can find out the work that God maketh from the beginning to the end." Ecclesiastics 3:11.

Prayer: Lord, forgive us for not being grateful for all that you have made.

🍷 97

God doesn't want me to understand His entire plan, which is His to know and work out. Many people search and study space to try and find the answers about how life began. They even spend a lot of money sending space ships out amongst the stars to try and find new life out there. It is something that has captured the imaginations of men for hundreds of years. Instead of actually travelling into outer space, they have written stories about what they imagine it could be like. Our quest for knowledge starts with Adam and Eve and I am grateful that while they are searching, solutions to other issues in our lives are found.

For me personally, I really am happy, to wait until I get to Heaven and then ask God about all the mysteries that elude me now.

"Neither is there any creature that is not manifest in his sight: but all things *are* naked and opened unto the eyes of him with whom we have to do." Hebrews 4:13.

Prayer: Lord, we are grateful that you know all the answers to space, time, and matter.

 98

If I was asked what I needed less of, my answer would have to be nothing! I need more contact with humans, more inspiration, more Bible Study, not less in order to keep writing. I need more challenges to teach me new things and expand my imagination. As farmers, we can always use more money and definitely more rain to revive the ground after this long drought.

We so often say that we need less stress, even less of the good things in life, but all these things make our lives full and colourful and without them our lives would be empty. It's the combination of all these things that creates growth, strength, knowledge, and gives us the power to move forward.

There have been many times when I have prayed for less stress and I have experienced such periods and found myself being bored very quickly. I know, we all dream of a life that resembles the Garden of Eden, but we destroyed that reality by wanting our own way, not God's way.

"All we like sheep have gone astray; we have turned everyone to his own way;" (Isaiah 53:6a).

With modern life being so stressful, what I think most of us need is more thankfulness, less complaining about the things that we already have, particularly in Australia. There are those who are in great need, and therefore, we also need more giving and less taking by those who can. So, I need more help (not less) from God's spirit to get me through the day.

"In everything give thanks: for this is the will of God in Christ Jesus concerning you." (1 Thessalonians 5:18)

Prayer: Help me, Lord, to depend on you more and more each day.

🍷 99

I've decided that I am allergic to bad, sad, and hyped up news. With the invention of social media, we have all become part of the news feed whether we like it or not. Regardless of the source; television, Facebook, newspaper, or books, anything that falls into these categories needs to be avoided.

Now, even I know that this is very unrealistic in today's world. We are force-fed this sort of information and, unlike my physical food allergies, I cannot avoid them, so I need an antihistamine. I'm not sure that even that returns the appetite quickly but at least it will stop me from dying.

What is the antihistamine for the bad news feed? It's found in Philippians 4:8

> **"Finally, brethren, whatsoever things are true, whatsoever things *are* honest, whatsoever things *are* just, whatsoever things *are* pure, whatsoever things *are* lovely, whatsoever things *are* of good report; if *there be* any virtue, and if *there be* any praise, think on these things."**

Prayer: Lord, we all have a responsibility to make sure that we eat and are dishing up is good quality spiritual food. Guide us in our endeavours, please.

🍷 100

Some traditions are good, but of course, they may not be good for everyone. On Good Friday we have had a tradition of eating Hot Cross Buns because they remind us of the cross and what Jesus did there for us. We have traditionally eaten Lamb for dinner as this reminds us that Jesus was the Lamb of God, the perfect sacrifice for our sins. It was also more convenient as we have always been sheep graziers.

> "For if by one man's offense death reigned by one; much more they which receive abundance of grace and of the gift of righteousness shall reign in life by one, Jesus Christ.)" Romans 5:17

While these things are good to help us remember the events of Good Friday what really is important is that we remember the Word of God in our hearts. If we cannot celebrate any day without the trappings then they are occupying a place they were never intended for. I no longer can eat Hot Cross Buns, but I never have to celebrate Good Friday without knowing scripture, and that is a good thing

Prayer: Lord, it is better that I talk to you each day than to remember you only on special days.

101

At Easter, we remember that Jesus died on the cross and rose again to save us from our sins. Just like birthdays, Anzac Day, and Christmas we have special traditions here in Australia that help us remember and celebrate. Other countries have their traditions which are often different to ours.

We have never been big fish eaters in this family. However, we have had fish on the table at times to remind us that Jesus wants us to go out and tell others about why He died for all humanity.

> "Go ye therefore, and teach all nations, baptizing them in the name of the Father, and of the Son, and of the Holy Ghost:" Matthew 28:19

Prayer: Even while I stay at home, Lord, please make me a fisher of men for you.

🍷 102

There is that saying, "the only exercise that some people get is jumping to conclusions". One night I had a nightmare. It revolved around my son having an accident. Now I don't normally take dreams to be premonitions, but, as he had not had his license for long, when I woke up at 1.15 in the morning, finding him not home yet, I jumped to the conclusion that my dream was one. I worked myself into a stew and waited for him to arrive home. He did, of course, at 2 am, parking his vehicle in the shed with no idea of what was going on in my head.

What I should have done is spend more of that time in prayer for friends and family. I did, a little, but seriously just not enough.

"Casting all your care upon him; for He careth for you." 1 Peter 5:7

Prayer: Lord, help me to remember that I can take all my cares and worries to you no matter what time it is

🍷 103

There is a saying that says: "jump to it and get on with the work". Today started out with me feeling a little down. So, to do something about it, I decided to sort out a cupboard and clean a certain messy room that was not really up to scratch, hence the "jump to it and get on with the work."

The bible tells me:

"Whatsoever thy hand findeth to do, do _it_ with thy might; for _there is_ no work, nor device, nor knowledge, nor wisdom, in the grave, whither thou goest." Ecclesiastes 9:10

It doesn't matter what it is that we find to do, small, medium or large, we need to do it well and with energy. Today's jobs, even though they were small, gave me a sense of achievement and made me feel so much better than I did the other morning. So, it's definitely better to jump, to it, not conclusions.

<u>*Prayer:*</u> Lord, help me to jump to it and work for you so that others will see your love for them.

♟ 104

Even when we accept the gift of His sacrifice, our "present" must be disturbed in order to improve our future. We must clean out our lives, and things will get messy, as we struggle to live in an imperfect world and learn how to do things differently to the way we are used to, but oh, what a wonderful future we have waiting for us in Heaven.

There will be sadness and grief over all sorts of things but our futures are filled with hope because we have come to Jesus individually at the foot of the cross, not just waved the palm leaves with the crowd. Even though we might not understand all that God has in store for our lives, we have that special hope that only comes because Jesus is our King.

"Beloved, now are we the sons of God, and it doth not yet appear what we shall be: but we know that, when he shall appear, we shall be like him; for we shall see him as he is." 1 John 3:2.

<u>*Prayer:*</u> I thank you for everything that you have in store for me because even though I don't know what it is, You know what is exactly right for me.

♟ 105

Most correspondence today is done through cyberspace, i.e. email, however, when we first moved to the farm, we had no internet and made very few trips to town, so there was always great excitement when an actual handwritten letter arrived. My mother was very good at letter writing and would often send a letter just so the kids had something to look forward to. During our weekly telephone conversations, she would generally mention if she had sent one.

One day, as we were driving to the mailbox at the front gate which is a one-and-a-half-kilometre drive from the house, one of the boys said: "I hope we have a letter in the box today." Ouch, I thought, mum didn't mention that she had sent a letter for the boys. So, as I drove along, I prayed "God only you can do something here."

We arrived and there was "mail" for the boys and as I said thank you, God, it reminded of the promise found in Isaiah 65:24,

"And it shall come to pass, that before they call, I will answer; and while they are yet speaking, I will hear."

God had known that the boys would like to receive a letter on that particular day, and had prompted my mother to write one, several days in advance so that it would arrive on time. I even feel that He allowed her to forget to mention it in order to surprise me and the boys and give us reassurance of just how much He cares about us.

Prayer: Only a God that knows all things and cares very deeply for all of His creation as individuals would go to all that trouble. I praise your name, oh Lord.

106

There have been times when I have felt like a prisoner in my own home. There was a time when I was laid up with a sore foot which would not allow me to drive, and as we live twenty minutes out of town, there is no other way for me to go places.

Yes, I was a bit like the Israelites, grumbling about my confinement. As I plan to do something that will take me away from home, there appears a health issue that stops me in my tracks. So, I have been asking God to show me what my real calling is. Do I stay at home, as a prisoner for Him? Learning to trust Him to send people to me instead of me going to them, or doing without people all together, is a tough lesson. I like to socialise and we get very few visitors here.

"I, therefore, the prisoner of the Lord, beseech you that ye walk worthy of the vocation wherewith ye are called, with all lowliness and meekness, with longsuffering, forbearing one another in love; Endeavouring to keep the unity of the Spirit in the bond of peace. *There is* one body, and one Spirit, even as ye are called in one hope of your calling;" Ephesians 4:1-4

Prayer: Lord, please make me patient, content, and an instrument for you while I am at home or out and about.

107

I wrote a story a few years ago, about a walk along a beach. During that walk, we came across a little girl and her father building a sandcastle. It was nearly finished, and dad was building a moat to be filled with water once the tide came in close enough. However, this little girl was impatient, and she was dancing at the water's edge waving to the waves, trying to entice them to come in and fill the moat right there and then. Every time I think about this little girl it makes me smile. It was such a cute thing for her to do.

I wonder if God smiles at us when we try to do the same thing as this little girl. Do I hear you say: "But we are adults, we know better, you cannot force waves to come in and fill a hole by waving your arms about?" Do we really know better? How many times do we make plans to do something and then tell God we are going to do it, often without even asking Him about them first? Some of us even tell God we are never going to do something.

"Whereas ye know not what *shall be* on the morrow. For what *is* your life? It is even a vapour, that appeareth for a little time, and then vanisheth away. For that ye *ought* to say, If the Lord will, we shall live, and do this, or that." James 4:14-15

Prayer: Lord, help me to remember to come to you first before making our plans.

♈ 108

People ask me why I married a farmer, particularly after they find out that I don't particularly like animals or farming. My response is: "When I was a teenager, I told God that I would never marry a farmer and He just smiled and said 'We'll see."

Of course, He knew that the man He had for me was my husband. Even as we made plans to get married, I had visions of us leaving the farming industry behind and going into to a formal ministry venture.

What I realize now is that I wouldn't have made a very good minster's wife, and that I had so much to learn before I could even consider such a thing.

Another thing God needed to teach me was that there are many forms of ministry and they are not always clothed in suits, uniforms, or gowns.

"For my thoughts *are* not your thoughts, neither *are* your ways my ways, saith the LORD. Isaiah 55:8

Prayer: Lord, your ways are a mystery to me, help me to trust you, so I can someday see the wonderful things you have for me.

109

Many words together make a sentence, many sentences make a story and in my case, many stories make a book. I enjoyed the experience of writing my first book, because I received a lot a feedback and encouragement. With the second book, I found it harder, because the feedback that I received was much more disjointed. My third book was a completely different experience altogether.

My major concern in all cases was to make sure that my many words are words of encouragement and truth. That was the wonderful thing about writing my first book, my mother's wisdom and insight was invaluable in making sure that I was kept on the straight and narrow.

"Therefore exhort one another, and build each other up, even as you also do." 1 Thessalonians 5:11.

There are many other people who are able to do just as good, or even, a better job than I can, however, I do know that even though I am only a small piece in the greatest jigsaw puzzle it is an important piece.

Prayer: Lord, I marvel at how your plan would not be complete without each and every person being a part of that plan.

110

When I talk about who I am today, it always makes me think about who I was in the past. I have been a daughter, a wife, a young mum, a working mum, a stand-in mum, a housekeeper, teacher, volunteer, reader, gardener, a bookkeeper, a secretary, and a go-for - that is probably not a real word, but it was a real job. Above all these things, I have been, and still am today, a child of God. He has used all the situations in my life, all the jobs that I have done, and all the people that I have met, to make me who I am.

So, who am I today that is different from my past? I am all these things still, as well as being a writer. I love writing! There may be even more stories written if I find some source of inspiration.

I always pray that someone will be encouraged by what I write. Why? Because during my past I have needed lots of encouragement to become the person I am today. It's a case of wanting to thank those in my past by helping those in my present by passing it forward.

Romans 8:28 says: "And we know that all things work together for good to them that love God, to them who are the called according to *his* purpose."

Prayer: While I will not always manage to do what *I* intended, God, you are in control, and you will work out *your* purpose.

🍷 111

Minimalistic is a great way to live if you can. After all, it allows us to be environmentally friendly, saves us money, reduces our workloads, and gives us time to spend with our loved ones. In our current, western, social structure, it can seem like a pipe dream. There are, of course, many countries where there are not many, if any, material trappings and yet the people, and particularly the children, are able to be happy playing with whatever they happen to have on hand.

Jesus also liked to keep things simple. After all, he didn't own property or many material goods.

"And a certain scribe came, and said unto him, Master, I will follow thee whithersoever thou goest. And Jesus saith unto him, The foxes have holes, and the birds of the air *have* nests; but the Son of man hath not where to lay *his* head." Matthew 8:19-20.

Even when we preach the word of God it is important to keep things simple and minimalistic so there is no room for confusion. Jesus wants us to be able to preach the word in such a manner that even children are able to understand the extent of His love, care, and plans for their lives. If we complicate what we say or do, we leave ourselves open to misinterpretation and this will make it easier for those we are trying to teach to be led astray.

"And said, Verily I say unto you, Except, ye be converted, and become as little children, ye shall not enter into the kingdom of heaven." Matthew 18:3

Prayer: Lord, may I always share the gospel by keeping it real and simple.

112

Each new day starts with a golden glow that promises good things and fulfilled plans. This, of course, is not always the way it works out. Things happen, changing the outcomes of the day and even the days to come.

When this occurred recently, I found myself trying to decide if the events were, in fact, the guiding hand of the Lord, or static from the devil to thwart His plans. Memories came to me of other instances where people have come up against a barrier to their plans, pushed through them, and still found blessings anyway. I have to wonder if I am just not being determined enough to carry out what I believe in, or am I being guided by God to stay where I am because He wants to protect me from some unknown disaster or trial.

In the New Living Translation Psalm 20:4 says

"May he grant your heart's desires and make all your plans succeed."

But the Holman translation says:

"May He give you what your heart desires and fulfill your whole purpose."

Prayer: Lord, I know that you love me, faults and all, and if I make mistakes the outcome will still be good.

🍷 113

Today I was able to spend time with some friends, face to face. We shared morning tea, lunch, and fellowship, and it was good.

It amazes me how so many times in life, once you take a step, you suddenly start to feel inadequate for the position. Sometimes, on a purely practical basis, I should not have even considered putting my hand up for jobs. In the past, vertigo attacks made making a commitment sort of hard for me, as traveling to distant towns and functions was difficult. So, stepping out in faith was not just about being able to do the job, but also about being able to get to places, and having someone to travel with me.

We are told in Matthew 28:19,

"Go ye therefore, and teach all nations, baptizing them in the name of the Father, and of the Son, and of the Holy Ghost:"

And sometimes that whole world is very close to home.

Prayer: Lord, help me to step out in faith, even when circumstances make it difficult.

🍷 114

The news comes to us in so many different ways these days. A long time ago, you would only get news from a person who had travelled many miles to bring it to you. Kings and Rulers would post notices on billboards to let people know what they had to do. Then, we progressed to newspapers and radios. Now we have television, phones, computers, newspapers, and iPads but they still tell us the same news, often over and over again.

When John the Baptist started telling people that the Messiah was about to come, it was good news.

"The voice of one crying in the wilderness, Prepare ye the way of the Lord, make his paths straight." Mark 1:3.

When Jesus told the people how to have their sins forgiven, that was good news too.

"But to all who did receive him, who believed in his name, he gave the right to become children of God," John 1:12.

When Jesus healed the blind, crippled and sick, these people went out and told others the good news. **John 9**.

On the other hand, when Jesus told the church leaders of His time that they were not doing the right thing, that was bad news and they didn't like it. They wanted to stone him.

"Then took they up stones to cast at him: but Jesus hid himself, and went out of the temple, going through the midst of them, and so passed by." John 8:59.

Prayer: Lord, let us repeat the good news enough without making people sick of hearing it.

🍷 115

This morning, there are some fruits of the labour that my husband put into a vegetable garden, on the table, and I thought how nice would it be if we could see those other fruits of the labour that we put into our family, friends, and strangers? The labours I am talking about are prayers, and those things that we do in the name of our God, Lord, and Saviour.

You might say that we do see what our children are like but not all parents see the final outcome. It is hard to know what children are hiding deep down. There are many people though, that we may meet casually, and we be prompted to pray for. You know those people, the driver in front of you who is obviously in a big hurry and you know that if they don't slow down an accident is a high probability. Have you ever stood at the sink and been prompted to pray for a friend, but you never find out why or what the outcome was?

"But thou, when thou prayest, enter into thy closet, and when thou hast shut thy door, pray to thy Father which is in secret; and thy Father which seeth in secret shall reward thee openly." Matthew 6:6.

Prayer: Lord, Thank you that even though I might not know the results of what I do here and now, one day I will.

🍷 116

I sometimes wonder what our soldiers in World War One snacked on? From what I have been told, Beef Jerky was something that was common. My son has decided that he likes this snack, which has no doubt been improved, and certainly I understand that the packaging has improved.

As adults, there are a lot of things that we have no choice about doing. This is something that is impossible for young children to understand. It often comes as a shock to young adults as they realize that there are certain things that just have to be done regardless as to how you feel about it.

Many of these young soldiers were given no choice about going to war, but they were adult enough to step up to the plate and did what had to be done for the loved ones at home, and all future generations.

Snacks are meant to be something you eat in order to get to the next meal, but many of these men had to survive on these snacks alone. As we remember our soldiers this week, I have to ask myself; would I have to courage and determination that all these people showed?

"Greater love hath no man than this, that a man lay down his life for his friends." John 15:13

Prayer: Lord, we thank you for the courage you gave our ANZACs and for the sacrifice that they made so that we would have the lifestyle we enjoy today.

117

As I wandered around Sydney recently, I noticed, particularly at the Railway Stations, that they were using orange for their logo and safety jackets. It stood out for two reasons; one, it was different and two, because it was bright.

I'm told that when my grandfather, who grew up in a Christian home, made his own commitment to Christ, the world seemed to be a much brighter place to be. While I understand it would not be an experience that everyone would have, it is nice to know that it is for some.

"And I saw a new heaven and a new earth: for the first heaven and the first earth were passed away; and there was no more sea. And I John saw the holy city, new Jerusalem, coming down from God out of heaven, prepared as a bride adorned for her husband. And I heard a great voice out of heaven saying, Behold, the tabernacle of God _is_ with men, and he will dwell with them, and they shall be his people, and God himself shall be with them, _and be_ their God. And God shall wipe away all tears from their eyes; and there shall be no more death, neither sorrow, nor crying, neither shall there be any more pain: for the former things are passed away. And he that sat upon the throne said, Behold, I make all things new..." Revelation 21:1-5

Prayer: Lord we thank you that one day we will have a new world which will be different and bright.

♈ 118

There are very few things in this world that are perfect. I know that, in some cultures, certain things have a deliberate mistake in them for the express purpose of reminding us that life here on earth is not perfect, that we all make mistakes and we should accept life as such.

It doesn't matter what it is that we make as a human being there will be faults, imperfections, and mistakes made. What is important, is that we do not allow them to be an overwhelming burden. Yes, I know I am just as guilty as the next person. I remember even recently having a discussion with God about how many mistakes I make and how his disciples didn't make such blunders. He was quick to remind that yes, they made big mistakes, but because I could see through the word that He had given us how they were still used by Him to work His plan, they didn't seem to be as huge. What I needed to remember, was that I could not see how God Himself would be working His bigger plan through me and those around me.

Psalm 18:30 says: "*As for* God, his way *is* perfect: the word of the LORD is tried: he *is* a buckler to all those that trust in him."

Proverbs 16:9 "The heart of man plans his way, but the Lord establishes his steps." (ESV)

Prayer: Lord, may I remember to let you direct me regardless of the plans I have made.

119

When we look at a reflection, what we see is a mirror image of the real thing. It is often blurred a little, particularly if the surface reflecting isn't completely smooth. It isn't always an exact copy and it doesn't matter if we are looking through water or glass, it will still be a distortion of the real thing. I think Paul understood this, and it seems to me that it could be why he says in 1 Corinthians 13:12,

> **"For now we see through a glass, darkly; but then face to face: now I know in part; but then shall I know even as also I am known."**

When it comes to reflection on past events or our personal lives, it can be a good or bad thing. One of the first things we are taught during our teacher training, is to reflect on how the lesson went, and how it can be improved for the next time around. This is something that is important for all the things that we organize, regardless whether it's a family dinner, meeting, or function. Some improvements can be made once we have worked out what things could have been done differently. If we are reflecting on our lives too much and we see only the bad things, reflection can be a very bad thing, only because it often can lead to depression and despair. We need to make sure that we reflect on the good as well.

Prayer: Lord help me to reflect on your word, this is a way to understand how to do things better in the future.

120

I was thinking about the Knights of the Round Table, which was round in order to give every Knight equal status; no one would end up at the "head" of the table because there wasn't one. Of course, there is always a "head" or leader of any group, and in this case, it would have been King Arthur. Equality within a group is helped when, not only the leader, but each member of the assembly, treats everyone with the same respect and courtesy, which is apparently what happened.

It has nothing to do with what duties have to be carried out by any member of that organization. Each member must have a different function, otherwise, nothing would ever be done effectively. Treating a cleaner or tea lady (do they have those anymore?) with the same respect as the President or the Finance Officer will make a workplace happier, healthier, and make a business, group, or organization go places fast and furiously.

It also reminds me that God made us all equal in His sight. He loves each one of us, not only because we are part of His family, but because He *made* us.

"There is neither Jew nor Greek, there is neither bond nor free, there is neither male nor female: for ye are all one in Christ Jesus." Galatians 3:28

Prayer: Lord, I know that you have a different job for each of us to carry out while we are here on earth, and that will be revealed to each one of us, at the right time, in God's special way.

121

What is the saying about a dog chasing its tail? It goes around and around and gets nowhere.

Life is never straight forward, well not for many of us it appears. Some days, I just seem to go around in circles and accomplish very little, which usually means they are filled with requests from other members of my family requiring my assistance. So, on these days, it's not that I haven't achieved anything, but the things that I wanted to do are not being completed.

When I was younger, and the children were smaller, it seemed that morning would arrive and it was "get the kids to school, get to work, come home, get dinner, kids to bed, housework and fall into bed yourself" only to repeat the exact same routine the next day. Weekends only varied by the fact that the work factor became housework that wasn't finished during the week, and getting kids to school, was replaced by sporting events or church.

It would appear that even King Solomon realized that life was a bit of a roundabout at times.

"Vanity of vanities, saith the Preacher, vanity of vanities; all *is* vanity. What profit hath a man of all his labour which he taketh under the sun? *One* generation passeth away and *another* generation cometh: but the earth abideth for ever." Ecclesiastes 1:2-4.

Prayer: Lord, I thank you that you do not "chase your tail". I praise you God, you are the beginning and the end, and always moving forward to eternity.

122

A good "rule of thirds" photograph has features being placed at one-third across the photo or the horizon being placed one-third from the top or bottom the screen. What about life, though, is there a rule of thirds, which can be applied to our existence? There are twenty-four hours in a day. When I was growing up, we were told that we should spend about eight of those sleeping, eight working and eight relaxing, developing relationships, worshipping, and enjoying our hobbies.

Now, I suspect that if we were to examine the timetables of most people in society today, we would find that they have very different timelines. I remember when my children were little, I was lucky to get six hours of sleep a night. What does God have to say? This covers our resting.

"Be still, and know that I *am* God: I will be exalted among the heathen, I will be exalted in the earth." Psalm 46:10

This encourages us to work to the best or our ability.

"Whatsoever thy hand findeth to do, do it with thy might; for there is no work, nor device, nor knowledge, nor wisdom, in the grave, whither thou goest." Ecclesiastes 9:10

And this gives us an idea of what might be a good idea to do with the rest of our spare time.

"With good will doing service, as to the Lord, and not to men:" (Ephesians 6:7)

Challenge: Remember that rest, work, and service, are a good way to divide up, not only our days, but our lives.

🍷 123

We have a bird that keeps banging at our laundry window. It seems to be such a silly thing for it to do. Sometimes they are trying to get to the insects that are on the inside of the window, on other occasions, they are just attacking themselves as they think their reflection is another bird.

There are times when I find myself doing the same thing, not literally of course, but spiritually. I am guilty of bashing myself up, thinking that if I work hard enough, I will be able to solve my problems. There are times when God has made me wait for His answers but they have always come. Sometimes I have had to wait two years, six years, and even thirty years, but He has always answered.

There are times when I need to just wait for the Lord to answer me. Yes, I know that sometimes He will say 'No' and it is at these times that I find myself still bashing away at the window, trying to get what I want, not what He wants.

"Wait on the LORD: be of good courage, and he shall strengthen thine heart: wait, I say, on the LORD." Psalm 27:14.

Prayer: Lord, help me to know when you want me to wait, and when you are saying no.

124

While working in the bedroom the other day, I wondered why the door of the wardrobe would not stay closed. It has been moved each time we relocated, stood up to the abuses of small five children and numerous grandchildren, so, was I surprised when I discovered that the door had come unhinged? Not really! You see I knew that the hinge was getting loose, and I didn't do anything to fix it.

Thinking about this, I wondered if many people think that society is a bit the same way – unhinged. What does it mean to be unhinged anyway? It means that things don't work properly. I ask you, is our society working properly? Do we care enough about people to respect their property? Some people do, absolutely, but those who rob and destroy don't. Do we care enough about people being abused? Some do, but those who use violence against their fellow men, women, and children, here at home and overseas, don't. Do we look out for each other? Again, some do, but those greedy people who take from the poor just to make themselves rich, don't.

Yes, I think that our society is a bit like that wardrobe door, it is unhinged. How did it get like that? Most likely in much the same way as that wardrobe door. We failed to notice that it was falling apart, or, if we did, we were too busy to do anything to fix it.

"Thou shalt love thy neighbour as thyself…" Leviticus 19:18b

Prayer: Lord, help us to keep our eyes on you so we do not fall apart.

125

What is special about 12 o'clock? It is special because at 12 midnight we start a brand-new day. Most of us are still very much in slumber land at that time, so we don't always notice its silent entry into our lives. A brand new day allows a brand new start. We can leave the troubles of the previous day behind us and look forward to starting over.

The other time that 12 o'clock occurs is midday, this signals the height of the day, the beginning of the afternoon. We are heading down towards evening. Some of us start to be concerned if a certain number of our duties have not been complete by noon. When I was younger, midday indicated that it was time for me to start doing relaxing things for myself or the children. These would be such things as craft or sewing. The mornings were usually taken up with housework, washing, and cleaning.

I was thinking back to what someone said recently. "Today isn't the end of the world, because it's already tomorrow in Australia". So, this made me think about what time it will be when Jesus returns. I'm thinking that we will be able to say 12 o'clock. It will no doubt be 12 o'clock somewhere, and it will signal the beginning of a beautiful, brand-new, eternal day.

"But of that day and *that* hour knoweth no man, no, not the angels which are in heaven, neither the Son, but the Father." Mark 13:32.

No matter when it is; it will signal a brand-new day.

<u>**Prayer:**</u> I thank you for all the brand-new starts that you give us.

126

Some people like to collect things. The only collection that has any real meaning for me, comprises of the lessons that God has taught me. We have all been blessed in one way or another. Some of us have been blessed with struggles and trials that make us stronger and able to empathize with people around us. Others with, what appears to be, prosperity and goodwill. Many people seem to think that:

"Jesus Christ the same yesterday, and today, and forever." Hebrews 13:8

Means we will all be treated the same way. So, what works for me will work for you.

There is something that these people have missed. God has made us all differently. This continues to blow my mind every time I think about this. Because we are made differently, we all react differently and God knows this. If you were able to ask the mother who has given birth to the largest family (67 surviving children!), I'm sure she will tell you that each one of her children was different.

To be able to learn these lessons, I have had to learn to listen to Him. His messages have come through so many different ways.

"He that hath ears to hear; let him hear." Matthew 11:15.

Prayer: I pray that you will hear what God is trying to tell you.

127

We all have to face dark days. Those days will vary from the ones where everything seems to go wrong to those days when bad news sends your world into a complete spin.

"A Psalm of David. The LORD *is* my shepherd; I shall not want. He maketh me to lie down in green pastures: he leadeth me beside the still waters. He restoreth my soul: he leadeth me in the paths of righteousness for his name's sake. Yea, though I walk through the valley of the shadow of death, I will fear no evil: for thou *art* with me; thy rod and thy staff they

comfort me. Thou preparest a table before me in the presence of mine enemies: thou anointest my head with oil; my cup runneth over. Surely goodness and mercy shall follow me all the days of my life: and I will dwell in the house of the LORD forever." Psalm 23.

As we enter the valleys of life, we have no idea how dark, deep, and long they will be, but the best we can do is hold the hand of our Lord and walk forward in faith knowing that He will be with us all the way.

"Have not I commanded thee? Be strong and of a good courage; be not afraid, neither be thou dismayed: for the LORD thy God *is* with thee whithersoever thou goest." Joshua 1:9

Prayer: Lord, I praise you for never letting go of my hand.

128

One of the many things farmers have to think about, is the depth of soil in their paddocks or fields or how far down the moisture levels are.

How far down the water has managed to soak is important to farmers. How deep the good soil is, is also very important. Both these things are pretty much out of our control. The good topsoil can be removed from the higher places by wind and rain, and deposited on the lower valleys by the same elements.

Yes, we can help protect the paddocks by leaving or planting trees, but we cannot undo the work already done in a hurry. It takes time, years in fact.

The same thing happens with people. It takes years for them to grow in maturity. We would not expect a one-week old baby to talk, let alone have the knowledge that we have accumulated over our lifetime.

When people become Christians, we need to be just as patient, understanding, and tolerant, because they are still young in spirit. They will need time to grow, learn, and understand. Just as we cannot put old heads on young shoulders in the normal world, so, we cannot put old spiritual heads on young spiritual shoulders.

How much depth and maturity they will develop is also pretty much out of our hands, because it is only God who waters and tends the fields of our spiritual lives.

"So then neither is he that planteth anything, neither he that watereth; but God that giveth the increase." (1 Corinthians 3:7).

<u>**Prayer:**</u> Thank you, Father, for making me grow as a person.

 129

Cooking a good meal is hard work, and then there is cleaning up to be done afterward. If you are the cook, putting all that hard work into a meal, it can be upsetting when it isn't eaten, or is just toyed with. In some countries, I understand that if you add anything, such as salt, pepper, or sauce you are insulting the cook. I also understand that in other countries it is appropriate to make, what we consider in Australia to be, rude noises, after a meal in order to show appreciation. The thing is, any meal is something that a lot of love and effort has been given to, to feed us and it is easy to make these wonderful cooks feel unappreciated or insulted.

Yet, how often do we do the same to God, we ignore the love and care that He shows us on a daily basis. Sometimes we are even unaware of just what we are doing.

"Consider the ravens: for they neither sow nor reap; which neither have storehouse nor barn; and God feedeth them: how much more are ye better than the fowls?" Luke 12:24

Some people reject everything that Jesus has done for them.

"He that rejecteth me, and receiveth not my words, hath one that judgeth him: the word that I have spoken, the same shall judge him in the last day." John 12:48.

Prayer: God, you care for us in many ways and often in ways that we may never know about, thank you, Lord.

130

My favourite drink is tea. In fact, it could be said that I might be addicted to it. I do occasionally prove this to not be the case as I have been known to go a whole day with only one or two cups.

When we think about drinking, we think about refreshment, relaxing after a long day at work, or just having fun with friends and family. This is often with some variety of alcoholic beverage. Of course, there are those that abuse the whole concept. We see reports on the news most weekends telling sad stories of bad behaviour, fights, car accidents, and lives ruined because of the abuse of such substances.

I decided early on in life to remain a "teetotaller" based on the knowledge that my great grandfather was, for part of his life, addicted to alcohol. Once he gave control of his life to Jesus, he was able to give up the drink, and live a life that was productive in business, and service of his God and church.

In his first letter to Timothy, Paul instructs him to stop drinking water and take a little wine for his stomach.

"Be no longer a drinker of water only, but use a little wine for your stomach's sake and your frequent infirmities." 1 Timothy 5:23.

It appears that there was a problem with the quality of the water that was available and that the wine was to be used in order to help the ailment.

Prayer: Please, Lord, refresh my soul by filling me with your Holy Spirit.

131

When I had young children, and I had to get out of bed early, I would often just enjoy the peace and quiet that surrounded me. It was often the only time that I would have to myself. With up to six children in the house at one time, there was never any real peace during the day, even if I could get them to have a rest.

Even now if I wake early, I just like to lie in bed and enjoy the early morning noises. Now that we are living on the farm, there are very few mornings when there are no sounds to hear. If it's not the chooks cackling or the dogs barking, there will be some bird or other telling me that it's time I was up. I enjoy this time, just listening and talking to God. I talk about all sorts of things, from what I might write, dreams I have had during the night, fantasies I could easily desire, my children and their problems, and my own disappointments. It really is a great time to talk and be with the Lord alone, even if I am still in bed.

The bible tells us that Jesus made a habit of rising early and going somewhere quiet to pray and talk to His father in Heaven.

"In the early morning, while it was still dark, Jesus got up, left the house, and went away to a secluded place, and was praying there." Mark 1:35.
(NAS)

Prayer: Lord, I thank you for the peace and quiet of each morning when I can talk to you by myself.

132

When the children were small, life was very busy and noisy. After the children had gone to bed there was always a mountain of chores that needed doing, and, if I bailed out of doing them, my brain was too busy sorting through the chaos of the day to be peaceful. This often meant that it would take me some hours to go to sleep. Is it any wonder that I was frequently tired and exhausted the next morning?

As I turned thoughts, dreams, and problems over in my mind, I found it hard to hand things over to God and let them go. It wasn't that I didn't pray for them, I did, but often, I would pray in a way in which I was telling God how to fix the problems, instead of placing them at the feet of Jesus and leaving them there. It wasn't because I didn't want to, but it was something I found very hard to do. It has only been as I have grown in my faith and seen how God has worked in our lives, despite my instructions, that I have developed the confidence to allow God to work according to His strategy, not mine.

"For my thoughts *are* not your thoughts, neither *are* your ways my ways, saith the LORD." Isaiah 55:8

Prayer: Lord, thank you for giving me what was best for me regardless of my interference.

133

I was reading about some of the great preachers in our history and discovered that many of them had suffered from depression, just like me. Depression sucks the energy out of you and makes facing daily tasks and problems exhausting. I remembered that David had also suffered in a similar way. So many of the Psalms start out with David feeling vulnerable and lonely, but end with him praising the God and Lord of his life.

I am beginning to understand that depression isn't a sin, it's an emotion! Like all emotions, it can cause us to sin if we let it control us. Ephesians 4:26 tells us,

"Be ye angry, and sin not: let not the sun go down upon your wrath:"

These words can also apply to any emotion, happiness, joy, depression, and grief. What I had to realize was, that I cannot solve a problem by looking at *it*. I need to look to Jesus to help me manage my emotions.

"Looking unto Jesus the author and finisher of *our* faith;" Hebrews 12:2a.

Prayer: Lord, I pray that I remember that you have all the answers. Please help me to continue to look to you for the solutions.

134

It had been one of those days, that most of us have from time to time, where at every turn something went wrong. I was spending a lot of time in tears, or on the phone, trying to find out what was going on and not making much progress on whatever front I was working on.

Fortunately, the sun was out and there was a stiff breeze blowing. This meant that I could use the energy from the sun to freshen up my pillows, and the wind was able to dry my washing. It was one of the few things that brightened my day as the washing machine didn't spin the clothes out properly and it had to be hung out very wet.

All the stress and tears managed to suck out of me the very little energy that I had. I was constantly asking myself where I was going to get the energy to get through the day. Bedtime seems to be such a long way away. I knew that I would sleep well, and that the next day would be a new day and most likely many of the problems I was facing this day, would be solved. There was still the question of how I was to be energized right then and there. I was reminded of this verse.

"Take my yoke upon you, and learn of me; for I am meek and lowly in heart: and ye shall find rest unto your souls." Matthew 11:29

Prayer: Lord, teach me to come to you and allow you to harness my life's problems so I can find the energy to get through each day.

🍷 135

I'm pretty sure there are days when people don't want to see my face, particularly if I am tired, angry, or sad. As a mother, there are very few, if any, days when I can hide away from my family and the world. We, as humans, are very interested in faces, they help us to read people and understand how they feel. When people talk to us, if we can see their face, we are able to tell if they are serious or if they are trying to tease us.

Of course, humans have always been interested in faces. Even Moses wanted to see the face of God. He wasn't allowed to, though, because it would have killed him.

"And he said, I beseech thee, shew me thy glory. And he said, I will make all my goodness pass before thee, and I will proclaim the name of the LORD before thee, and will be gracious to whom I will be gracious, and will shew mercy on whom I will shew mercy." Exodus 33:18-20

Prayer: While I am quite happy not to see the face of God here on earth, I Thank you that one day I will see Him face to face, and that will be a very awesome experience.

🍷 136

Nothing frustrates us more than being controlled or directed by what society has named 'those faceless men'. They are the people who appear to make decisions without actually having any first-hand or practical experience of a given situation. Their solutions usually create many more problems than they were designed to solve.

The old-fashioned process of starting at the bottom and working your way up the ladder in order to understand an industry is not considered to be relevant anymore. Even getting physically involved in a situation in order to better understand the problems and issues is no longer the way things are done. It seems that if a book says that something will work then it will.

However, it still holds that sometimes, human theory doesn't work out in practice; God can still surprise us with very different answers to our problems.

I think of Peter and John when they were fishing all night. They caught nothing, but Jesus had a surprising answer for them because He knew exactly where the fish were. **John 21:5-6**. The answer was so amazing that John exclaims,

"It is the Lord." John 21:7.

Sometimes the answers we get to our problems will make us exclaim with the same amazement "It is the Lord".

Prayer: Lord, your solutions are sometimes surprising and simply amazing, beyond our comprehension. Lord, may we remember that you have the answers to every problem we face.

137

I had run out of sticky tape and I was in a hurry, so, I start searching, one drawer at a time. As I pulled open one particular drawer and looked down, there sitting on top was a spider. Now, I'm not really afraid of these creatures, but I pulled back quickly enough.

A quick surface look revealed that the said "sticky tape" wasn't to be found without things being moved around. No, I didn't poke around and do a thorough search. As I turned around, I spotted a new roll sitting right there on a shelf. I hadn't seen it lying there before probably because I was in such a hurry.

Fear is a powerful force. You can see it as the motivation behind what people do and say. It is also a force that will prevent people from doing what they should or would like to do.

Psalm 118:6 says: "The LORD *is* on my side; I will not fear: what can man do unto me?"

There have definitely been times when I have been frozen with fear myself and, thankfully, God has sent someone along to remind me of the truth.

"And fear not them which kill the body, but are not able to kill the soul: but rather fear him which is able to destroy both soul and body in hell." Matthew 10:28

Prayer: Help me, oh Lord, to remember that my eternity is in your hands and that is very precious.

138

I'm old enough to have had to attend Home Economic classes at school. For those that don't understand what I am talking about, they were classes to teach girls how to cook, sew, wash up, and carry out home duties. One of the units each year was Floral Art. Oh dear, I didn't pass with great marks. It was considered back then to be an essential skill for a homemaker. I just realized that we weren't taught gardening skills in those classes, hum – were the flowers supposed to appear by magic or was it considered the man's job to produce the flowers? I must confess to some memory loss on that front.

Floral Art, from my poor memory, had elements of proportion, balance, form, and sometimes, a theme. Some arrangements go as far as to tell a story.

Some people are able to live their lives according to these rules as well with proportion, balance, and form. Appling them to how much time they give to work, children, families, hobbies, and church. Some of us though, are a lot like me when it comes to floral art. I pick some flowers; pull off the unnecessary leaves, find a vase, fill it with water and plonk the flowers in. They still look great, they smell wonderful, particularly if I have cut roses or jonquils and they brighten up the whole room.

Prayer: Lord, like the flowers make a room feel brighter, help me to brighten up someone's life and make them feel a little better every day.

139

My family has so many allergy issues that I have been known to say that food is a "four-letter word" for me. I posted this once and someone said, "but it is a four-letter word", my response was, "each time I think about food I want to swear". I just shudder to think about what food might be available if I am ever confined to an institution.

I need to remember, though, that I can at least still eat. Many others cannot. I am blessed, simply because God selected Australia as the place for me to live. He also blessed me with the time that He selected for me. Had I been born in previous centuries I would have been very ill or died at a very early age! So, while the whole issue of food annoys me quite a bit, I have to remember on a daily basis that I am very blessed.

Of course, another thing that I need to remember is that while I need food to survive, it can be overindulged in. That will, and has, created other problems to be dealt with. Along with this, there is one other thing that I need to remember.

"And he humbled thee, and suffered thee to hunger, and fed thee with manna, which thou knewest not, neither did thy fathers know; that he might make thee know that man doth not live by bread only, but by every *word* that proceedeth out of the mouth of the LORD doth man live." Deuteronomy 8:3.

Prayer: Lord, while food can be a trial, you know exactly what I need.

140

As I thought about why we forget things, I realized that it is often because something else becomes more important. It can be the needs of children, grandchildren, or work to name a few. Why, you ask, would you walk away from a job when you know it has to be completed? You see, when people are busy, they have trouble waiting for things to happen. After all, another job shouldn't take more than ten minutes, and you should be back in plenty of time to finish off the previous job. The problem is, of course, that what starts out to be a ten-minute job often ends up being a twenty or thirty minute one.

Of course, this can happen on a spiritual level as well. How many times have you asked someone about their spiritual health and they have replied along the lines of 'I'm too busy to think about it just now' or 'I'll deal with that when I have more time'? I know I have come across some people who have said similar things to me. Sometimes, I myself have slipped into a situation where I have been too busy to give God and His plan for my life much thought. It doesn't mean that I have forgotten Him, but He has been pushed into the back of my mind for a short time.

So many times throughout scripture we are instructed to:

"........Love the Lord thy God with all thy heart, and with all thy soul, and with all thy strength, and with all thy mind; and thy neighbour as thyself." Luke 10:27 see also Matthew 22:37, Mark 12:30-31, Deuteronomy 6:5.

Prayer: Lord, trying to stay focused is hard sometimes but, Lord, please help to keep my eyes on you.

141

One of the most difficult jobs my husband has to do as a result of the drought is pull sheep free from the mud when they get stuck in the dam. Some people just cannot understand why they would be silly enough to get stuck in dams, particularly when there is water available at a water trough in the same paddock.

These sheep, however, are not really that different to people, are they? Some people, when they find themselves in desperate circumstances, move headlong into the situations that have consequences that they had not anticipated. They find themselves in circumstances that they are unable to get out of without the assistance of someone bigger, stronger, and more powerful.

There is someone who is bigger, stronger, and more powerful who can help them.

Psalm 40:1-2 "I waited patiently for the Lord and he inclined unto me and heard my cry. He brought me up also out of a horrible pit, out of the miry clay and set my foot upon a rock and established my goings."

Prayer: Thank you Lord Father for all the times that you have rescued me from the pits of trouble.

142

Some people seem to get themselves into trouble so often that you can be flabbergasted. Those of us standing on the sidelines of these peoples' lives sometimes shake our heads and wonder how they managed to get into such a mess. We can judge and debate about why they didn't take up other options that they had available. We can declare that we wouldn't get into the same mess and maybe we wouldn't but that is us, not them. We cannot know what we would do if we were that person, with their history, makeup, and emotional state.

There is a saying that goes something like: "But for the grace of God go I" and as I look back over my life so far, I have no idea how many times God has saved me from going in a different direction and heading down a slippery slope to some disaster.

One of the things that my mother used to repeat to me over and over again was, that no matter what I think is a good thing, God knows what is best. Yes, God will keep his eyes on me if I go my own way but the consequences will still have to be dealt with and I cannot expect God to put me back on the starting path where I went astray. It will take longer to get to where I need to end up, than it would have before.

"In all thy ways acknowledge him, and he shall direct thy paths."
Proverbs 3:6.

Prayer: Lord, remind me that you know better than I do about what is good for me.

143

My husband found a couple of plum trees on another property that we own. He picked a small quantity and brought them home. His plan was to feed them to the chooks, but I decided to have a go at making Plum Sauce. I have never been very good at this sort of cooking, but I was willing to give it a go. If the final product was no good, then the chooks could still eat them, even if it was in a different form.

As I was cooking the sauce, I reflected on how this could be related to our lives. Is it a wonder to anyone else that we start off being just plain people and then, as we grow up, we have various experiences that could be described as salt, sugar, vinegar, spice, or heat from the stove? These experiences help change us as people; our attitude to them will mould us into the sort of adults that we grow up to be. How is it that some people become mature, capable, and useful, while others just don't seem to be able to manage to even hold down a job, or cope with day to day activities? These are the mysteries of life.

God does not want us to break through the experiences of life, He wants us to grow strong and powerful.

> "As many as I love, I reprove and chasten. Be zealous therefore, and repent." Revelation 3:19,

You can also check out Hebrews 12:6 and Proverbs 3:12.

Prayer: Thank you, Lord, that you help us to grow through all the things we experience.

144

When I talk about mowing, I always say that I have been outside mowing the grass, not the lawn. Why? As far as I am concerned, my yard is not covered in lawn, it is covered in grass. What is the difference? you might well ask. In my mind, a lawn is made up of a particular type of grass and the whole area should be covered with the same variety. The large area that I consider to be my backyard is hardly covered with grass at all during long dry spells in the weather. It certainly is not covered with the same variety all over. In fact, it is also comprised of a large quantity, of what many people would consider, weeds. So, I am, from today, going to change my thinking and remember that all those different varieties of grass are all good for something. They help cover my ground and therefore there is no reason for me not to call it "Lawn".

My lawn is just like all the people in the world, we are all different. We have different coloured skin, personalities, skills, and interests, and we make the world a very interesting place to live in. God made us all with diverse abilities because He wanted us to contribute something different to the lives of those around us. Let us celebrate our differences not try and get rid of them.

"So, we, being many are one body in Christ, and every one member's one of another." Romans 12:5

Prayer: Lord, help me to remember that I am different because you made me that way for a reason.

145

While having lunch with a friend, we got talking about what Christians look like. We discussed how we often stereotype people. They should behave in a certain manner, say the right things all the time, and dress a particular way. We chatted about how we have polished up the cross that Jesus died on and concentrated only on the good things about the servants of God. We try to ignore their rough, tough exteriors and their disobediences, in other words, we have polished them up. These servants of God were tough, rough, and sinful. They made mistakes, sometimes big ones, but God loved them and used them for His glory despite all of their faults.

We often get very discouraged when we mess up and make mistakes. What we need to remember, is that we are human, and we all make blunders, and, despite all our faults, God still loves us and will use us to carry out His plan.

God knows all about our flaws, and, because He is in control of the world's history, He will use those flaws to His advantage, but we have to allow Him into our lives and let Him work through us. Over time, He will help change us so that some of the flaws will fade but that job will take a lifetime.

"Being confident of this very thing, that he which hath begun a good work in you will perform *it* until the day of Jesus Christ:" Philippians 1:6

Prayer: Lord, I ask that you continue to work through me, and in me, so that I will be able to work for you.

146

With the start of spring and some rain, the grape vine at the back of the house started to grow. It took only a few weeks, three to be precise, for the small green grapes to appear. If you saw these vines three weeks before, you may have even been convinced that they were dead and needed to be pulled out. One was even hidden in amongst some bushes that had suckered up around it. It was watered at the same time as the other vines but had not been able to get the same amount of sunshine. The difference in the progress of the two vines is very noticeable.

Have you ever wondered why sometimes things or people are taken away from us? Maybe sometimes it is not because they were bad or wrong, but maybe it is time for us to see Jesus more directly. It could be time for us to put on some new growth. Yes, the process can be painful and disconcerting, but God is faithful and He has a very good reason for making us stand more directly in His light.

Jesus tells us in John 15:1:

"I am the true vine, and my Father is the husbandman."

It is God who not only prunes the vine itself, but also tends the ground around through which the vine is growing. It is God who makes sure that we are exposed to the sun (Son) and that our lives are not hindered with overgrown rubbish plants around us.

Prayer: Next time something is removed from my life, help me to remember to look to you a little more closely.

147

We have a doorjamb, which is the designated recorder of the heights of our children and grandchildren, as they grow taller. It surprises me that the children still measure themselves against the marks that are there when they come home to visit. You have to smile as parents compare their children to themselves and their aunts and uncles.

Growing taller is only one sign that we are growing up. We have to grow inside as well. I often feel sad for those parents that do not experience this, for whatever reason, in their children. Yes, we all have days when we are frustrated with their behaviour, but in the end, they are alive, active, and capable. What more should we ask for, other than patience?

Of course, as adults, we do not stop growing either. We learn different things from our world, our children, and grandchildren. I must remember when it comes to growth, that if I compare myself to those around me, it will stunt my growth as a person.

"But grow in the grace and knowledge of our Lord and Saviour Jesus Christ to Him be the glory, both now and to the day of eternity. Amen." 2 Peter 3:18 (NAS)

Challenge: To grow up in the Lord and become more like Him by listening to His messages for me.

148

It is cold and wet outside, and I can laugh at the weather. Why? Because I have so many things that will keep me warm. Warm drinks, soup, and a wood fire heater help me to stay warm. I realize that not everyone is blessed with such comforts. Gratefulness is something that I don't exercise enough but I'm told that my quality of life would improve if I did.

1 Thessalonians 5:18 says "In everything give thanks: for this is the will of God in Christ Jesus concerning you."

And I know just like me, that many people find this verse hard to comprehend particularly when they are in the middle of a crisis or bad patch. Yet it is there as a directive from God Himself.

From my experience, I have found that it is often only in hindsight that we can see the good that comes from those dark days when we wanted to yell, "why me instead of Thank You Lord".

"And we know that all things work together for good to them that love God, to them who are the called according to *his* purpose" Romans 8:28.

<u>**Prayer:**</u> I thank you, Lord, for all the blessings that you have given to us.

🏆 149

Something that I have discovered during my life is that, if we obey our Lord and Saviour, He will lead us down paths that will strengthen us and teach us things that we may never have learned any other way.

Even when we are having a string of bad days, there will always be days among them when we will be able to laugh at something or find some small thing to be grateful for. It might be a flower that has bloomed, a hug from a child, or just a nice hot cup of tea.

While it is hard to do sometimes, we just have to look at the situation from a different angle to see a beauty, joy, and happiness that we could not see before.

Paul and Silas had bad days but, even when they were thrown into prison, they made an effort to praise God. They also shared the good news that Jesus loved the prisoners enough to die on the cross for them.

"And at midnight Paul and Silas prayed, and sang praises unto God: and the prisoners heard them." Acts 16:25

Prayer: "God help me to see something beautiful, happy, and lovely today, even if it is a bad day."

🍷 150

I have two boys, these boys are like chalk and cheese; one is quiet, the other outgoing. One day, when the boys were small, as we were leaving the Post Office, one of them noticed the cross that could be seen on top of a church one block away. "Why do churches put crosses on top of their buildings?" one of them asked. "To remind us that Jesus died so we can go to heaven", was my response.

The outgoing one asked, "What is Heaven like?" The quieter one responded with "A nice quiet peaceful place"

"Oh well, when I get there I'll noise it up" was the comeback from his brother. I smiled and thought "Yeah, I'm sure you will".

As with my boys, one was happy when things were quiet and peaceful, the other was happy to be running around and investigating his world, so their ideas of Heaven were very different. No matter how many times I read the descriptions of Heaven in Revelation, I have so much trouble being able to actually picture it. One thing is for certain, the Bible tells us:

"And God shall wipe away all tears from their eyes; and there shall be no more death, neither sorrow, nor crying, neither shall there be any more pain: for the former things are passed away." Revelation 21:4

Prayer: Lord, I thank you for the hope of Heaven, no matter what it is really like.

151

With the increased use of social media, I have been able to connect with people from all over the world. I am constantly impressed with the variety of personalities that seem to value my thoughts. We often only connect on a narrow spectrum. Some people I have actually met in person after making the initial contact through Facebook. I have to say that I have always approached such meetings with great caution, because I am well aware that what you see on an internet page could be very different to the reality. There are so many horror stories, about how people have been destroyed, that fear comes along with every possible meeting. Yet, I have also found many people to be encouraging, and I am sure that some of them, I will meet for the first time, in Heaven.

When we read the records of the early Christian church, we get to understand that not everyone got along. People were as diverse then as they are now. Yet, God was able to use all their personalities and differences to bring about the greatest change this world has known up to now. One day, the world will see the most magnificent change when Jesus returns. The differences that annoy us about others and our traits that annoy others will not matter then because we will be able to see how they are just part of the great blueprint of God

> **"For we are his workmanship, created in Christ Jesus for good works, which God prepared beforehand, that we should walk in them."**
> **Ephesians 2:10 (NAS)**

Prayer: Lord, when others annoy me, help me to remember that you made them with love and for a purpose.

🍷 152

Someone I know mentioned that they had visited a Psychic. They were told how old they would live to, and some other information about a loved one, that I could tell gave them some comfort. The conversation was prefaced with "I know you don't believe in them". The thing is, I do believe that some people have the ability to see such things, but, and here is the BIG but – I don't believe that the information should ever be relied on as being accurate. This is why:

These people are still human, and they are still able to misinterpret things, just as we ourselves misread the signs around us. If the information were always correct, then there would be no need for us to walk by faith. For instance, being told that you will live to a certain age, means that you don't have to worry about what you do, until that age is reached.

The problem here, is that it would be such a temptation to put off doing some very important things (like our relationship with Jesus) because you have been lulled into thinking that you have plenty of time to do them later. God wants us to be ready for His return at any moment. Our relationship with Him should not be put off until later.

"However, no one knows the day or hour when these things will happen, not even the angels in heaven or the Son himself. Only the Father knows." Matthew 24:36 (NLT)

Prayer: Lord, I thank you that you know what the future holds and you control it as well.

🍷 153

I was thinking about a backyard that we had at one of our houses during my childhood. Chrysanthemums of all different colours grew so well in a terraced section, below the chook yard, which was situated on a high area near the back fence.

What I didn't know, at the time, was that runoff from the chook yard was feeding the plants every time it rained. The plants were being fed all the time by the natural forces at work. I have no idea if this was a deliberate strategy by my parents, or if this was just a way to tidy up a barren area, and slow down the water flow during heavy rain. Regardless, this garden produced the best flowers I have ever seen in my life.

Thinking about this garden today, I realized that this garden is a good example of what should be happening in our lives. We should be fed spiritually from above. We need to read the word of God and let Him feed us. His power is much higher than ours, His knowledge greater than ours, and His love for us is more powerful than any human could give. As we constantly feed on His word, and grow strong and beautiful, we have a responsibility to share that love and knowledge with those who have no idea of who God is.

"But to do good and to communicate forget not: for with such sacrifices God is well pleased." Hebrews 13:16

Prayer: Lord, please let the love and knowledge you give me flow out to others so they too will know how wonderful you are.

♛ 154

These days, when I need help for Bible quotes, I often use the internet. If that is not available, I use a concordance, my Bible, or a Study Bible. There are so many different things that are now available for me, and it's only available due to the hard work of other people, who have put these resources together.

You know, sometimes we can get bogged down in our spiritual sources of help and inspiration. It is easy, for me at least, to rely on the same preacher, same author, and same teachers for my spiritual food. I'm a little afraid of having to do the hard work of making sure that what I read and hear is correct. I just want to be able to feed, and not have to sort stuff, but that is not the way God wants us to learn about Him. He wants us to listen and check and make sure that what we are hearing is truly from Him and not from the devil. Here on earth, we have to make sure that what we get is pure spiritual food because there are two forces at work here.

"Beloved, believe not every spirit, but try the spirits whether they are of God: because many false prophets are gone out into the world." 1 John 4:1

Prayer: Oh Lord, thank you that when we get to Heaven, everything will be perfectly sorted.

155

Home is where we are supposed to feel loved and safe, but sadly this is not the case for many people. I was fortunate, as a child, to have such an experience. We never had a house that we could call home, we moved on an average of once a year. When you move so many times, you need to find somewhere that represents home. For me, it was the hometown of my father and mother. They started their lives in Inverell, and, while my mother did leave for a few years, she returned and continued to live there until she went to work for the Salvation Army.

Inverell was also home because my father's parents lived there and we stayed with them during holiday trips "home". It was the centre that our lives revolved around. It didn't matter where we went to for work, Inverell was that constant centre. To us children, Grandma and Grandpa would always be there.

For those who have not had the security of being loved and safe here on earth, it is important to remember that there is a place where we will experience such a miracle. It is Heaven, where we will experience the joy of being completely loved and safe.

"And God shall wipe away all tears from their eyes; and there shall be no more death, neither sorrow, nor crying, neither shall there be any more pain: for the former things are passed away." Revelation 21:4

And one day, we will be home forever.

Prayer: Lord, please show those, who do not feel the security of human love, your perfect love for them.

156

Years ago, I was given an ornamental pot plant holder. While it wasn't very big, it still brightened up my lounge room. It was in the style of a classical Greek/Roman child holding an urn of some sort, into which, the plant was supposed to go. However, like many of my things, it was knocked over one day and the urn part broke. The pieces that broke off were too small to be glued back together. I didn't feel like throwing the whole thing out, so it stayed in the corner in its broken state – until I bought some artificial flowers to cover up the broken top.

You know many people that are broken, just like that ornament. Many people go out and buy all sorts of things to cover up their broken spirits. Things like make-up, new clothes, big homes, sports cars, and even self-improvement courses. The truth still is, though, they often still feel just as broken underneath.

"For God sent not his Son into the world to condemn the world; but that the world through him might be saved" John 3:17

When we read this verse, we are reading a promise from God to help broken people. However, because we live in a broken world, there is a brokenness that will remain until we reach Heaven. Yes, we are saved, and Jesus has made something beautiful out of that brokenness, but only in Heaven will we be completely healed. Isaiah 25:8 promises that:

"He will swallow up death in victory, and the Lord God will wipe away tears from off all faces..."

Prayer: Thank you, Lord, for the healing that you do for us now and will complete when we get to Heaven.

🍷 157

"Grandma I found this car!" The voice of my grandson breaks into my writing. He held out his hand and in his palm was the smallest car I have ever seen. It was such a small thing that it was no wonder that it had got lost in the first place. I'm surprised that it was even found.

This led me to think about just how small we are, each of us, in the body of Christ. We are only one person, one, in all those people that had faith in God from the beginning of time. Yet, no matter how small, and how insignificant we feel, God knows and loves us and will teach us in the unique way that He knows we will learn best. There will be times when we will feel lost and overwhelmed by the circumstances that we find ourselves in. Just like that small car that my grandson found, we will be found by God, and loved just as much as the person who is next to us, as we drive along the road of life.

"So we, *being* many, are one body in Christ, and every one members one of another." Romans 12:5

Prayer: Lord, thank you for reminding me when I am struggling to understand where my life plan is going, that even though I am as small as a cell, I am loved by my Heavenly Father.

158

I hear home calling. My mobile phone rings and as I look at my phone, I can see that the call is coming from home. I have been away for several weeks now. I love being with other members of my family and they have looked after me so well while I have been sick. However, now that I am starting to feel better, I WANT TO GO HOME. I want to sleep in my own bed, watch my own television, eat from my own pantry, and see my own garden. (No, I won't be able to do anything but I just want to go home).

These things are familiar, they are mine and I want them around me again. When I was sick, it didn't matter where I was, I just wanted to be cared for.

There is, of course, another home that one day will call me. The desire to be there is, of course, very different to what I am experiencing right now. I have never been there; all I know about the physical attributes of my real home is what I read in Revelation. I'm afraid my imagination just cannot put those words into any sort of picture that I can relate to. It is home to me because so many of my friends and family (particularly my mum) are already there waiting for me.

Besides, who wouldn't want to live in a perfect world forever? I know that I want to when my time comes. I also know, that when I have completed the work that God has for me to do here on earth, I will be really ready to go home, but for the present, I'd like to say with Paul:

"For to me, to live is Christ and to die is gain. But if *I am* to live *on* in the flesh, this *will mean* fruitful labour for me; and I do not know which to choose." Philippians 1:21-22.

Prayer: Lord, I thank you may I continue to love you until you call me home to Heaven.

♈ 159

I was out in the garden one day, when I was delighted to see an unusual sight. An echidna was heading under the house. I figured that he had decided that it was an acceptable place for him to hang out for a while. My husband had spotted him in the garden before this sighting and I have seen him again since.

I have to wonder how long he might hang around. It's not as if he will not be disturbed from time to time by the farm animals. So, I think he is only staying for a while, as he continues on the journey of life.

It reminded me of what Jesus said about His living arrangements:

"And Jesus saith unto him, The foxes have holes, and the birds of the air *have* nests; but the Son of man hath not where to lay *his* head." Matthew 8:20

Challenge: Just like the echidna, we are all passing through this world. Let us make sure that we make a good impression on our way.

♈ 160

Oh, the taste of something sweet and different, some might say naughty even. For a person on a very strictly controlled diet, these treats are rare, but extremely, and I do mean *extremely,* enjoyable. I must always be careful to make sure that, when I do indulge, that I stop at one or two.

As I enjoyed this particular treat this morning, I thought about how, growing up, we were taught to have strict spiritual diets. This is about how we behaved, what we read or watched, and the various activities that we participated in. It took me a long time to understand that the occasional treat was not going to hurt me. In fact, with the right approach, meaning that God goes with me, I now understand that sometimes these things, that fall outside the strict rules I grew up with, can often be opportunities to witness for Him.

Now, please don't get me wrong, Christ would never be honoured by our participation in some activities, and these, like my allergies, are always off limits. But we should not miss those, because our God is a generous God, who gives good gifts and a wonderful array of benefits to His children, and sometimes, like my sweet treat, that is going to be something special that tells us just how much we are loved by Him.

"Every good gift and every perfect gift is from above, and cometh down from the Father of lights, with whom is no variableness, neither shadow of turning." James 1:17

<u>Prayer</u>: Thank you for loving me, for allowing our lives here to be filled with good gifts.

🏆 161

I work from home these days. I am grateful that, despite my house not having all the finishing touches, we have a strong roof over our heads, and plenty of room for all my grandchildren to come and visit. However, there are times when I think our house is being underutilized because, like everything I own, I like to use it fully for the glory of God.

"For where your treasure is, there will your heart be also." Luke 12:34

There are many times when God puts our seemingly busy lives on pause and they seem to be underutilised just like my house.

Despite what you might think, it also takes the same amount of courage to trust God when He has pushed the pause button, as it does when the fast-forward button is on.

I have been thinking about how hard it must have been for Moses, when he returned to Egypt to rescue the Israelites, only to find that things were going nowhere fast. The mission appeared to be going nowhere. In fact, things seemed to be going badly, very badly. I imagine that his vision was that he would go to Pharaoh, ask him to allow the people to go, they would negotiate a deal and they would leave. But we know that God had very different plans.

"Be strong, and of a good courage, fear not, nor be afraid of them: for the Lord thy God, he it is that doeth go with thee, he will not fail thee, nor forsake thee." Deuteronomy 31:6

While my house isn't finished yet, I need the courage to glorify God in it, and I also know that I have one home that is completely finished, and, in that one, I will be praising Him forever.

"In my Father's house are many mansions:" John 14:2a

Prayer: Lord, may I always remember where my real home is.

♀ 162

I am proud: of my children for surviving the mistakes and muddle of being raised by me; of my father, and the progress that he has made to adjusting to life on his own; and of myself, for my own growth over the years of raising five children, working, and studying at the same time. As I thought about all these things, I realized that none of it happened without teamwork, people working together to make something happen. So, I am proud of the teamwork that goes to making life work.

Just like the way we have to live life, we often have to think outside the box to find the solutions for the problems that living in our world presents us with, but we have the greatest creative thinker there is, to help us all the time. We don't have to log onto the internet, make a phone call, or even travel great distances to find the answer. All we have to do is ask. We may not get the answer instantly but answer He will because He has promised.

"Ask, and it shall be given you; seek, and ye shall find; knock, and it shall be opened unto you:" Matthew 7:7

Prayer: Thank you, Lord, for all the ways you help us to solve the problems in this world, and that you are forever on our "team".

🏆 163

If you looked inside my fridge, you would find a variety of foods and treats. There are days when you would find things that shouldn't be there. Maybe I had been very busy for a while and I had not managed to clean it out.

Now, what is my fridge going to teach me about life? We all like to keep things locked away from the rest of the world, and, just as the fridge keeps my food at a safe temperature, in many cases not exposing everything to the world, is very necessary, in order to preserve myself. Yes, some of those things will be off, and really should be tossed out, but God will do that in His own good time.

"Lord, all my desire _is_ before thee; and my groaning is not hidden from thee." (Psalm 38:9).

After all, He is the one that is in control of my life. If you were able to see the things hidden in my life you will find that there is a great variety of things stashed away. They have been a result of the very different experiences, people, trials, and joys that have been part of my life. However, I know that God sees all those things that I don't want to show to the world because nothing is hidden from Him.

"For nothing is secret, that shall not be made manifest; neither _anything_ hid, that shall not be known and come abroad." Luke 8:17.

Prayer: Lord, only you can see all that is in my life and I am thankful that you love me anyway.

164

I look to my fingernails to get an indication of how healthy I am on the inside. When they are strong, I can usually say that I am in good health, when they chip, crack, and break, then there is usually something going on that is not right.

I put up with bad nails for years, thinking that that's just the way things were. It wasn't until I got my health sorted out, and my nails showed a great deal of improvement, that I realized that what I thought was normal, wasn't.

This got me thinking; what are the spiritual indicators of good health? What is it that fails to be strong when we get tired, lazy, or just spiritually ill? I think the fruits of the spirit start to chip, crack, and dry up and the first one of these to do so, is love.

"By this shall all *men* know that ye are my disciples, if ye have love one to another." John 13:35.

Prayer: Lord, may we continue to produce the fruits of the spirit by staying close to you.

165

When I was a child, we only had fireworks once a year, on what we called Bonfire Night. We enjoyed it so much. These days, when fireworks are part of every function, show, and festival, I find myself not enjoying them nearly as much. There was a time when life's little extras were given at birthdays and Christmas, but now, we have so many extras that we struggle to appreciate the things we have, let alone find joy in them.

Christmas was made special because you got to taste certain foods, drinks, and sweets. Easter time was a special time for Easter buns and chocolate. By making these things commonplace, we remove their specialty and the joy of experiencing them only once in a while.

I found joy recently in the birthday messages that I received from family and friends. They can only happen on my birthday and they brought me joy. Yes, in times of drought we experience joy when the rain finally falls, but it doesn't take long, when it continually rains and floods, for people to lose the joy of having rain fall. There is joy in being able to trust someone because these days, trust is something that is rare in people.

Finally, there is only one God that cares for me, that I can trust and that, I know, will never be ordinary, so I find joy in Him.

"Therefore, I tell you, do not worry about your life, what you will eat or drink; or about your body, what you will wear. Is not life more than food, and the body more than clothes? Matthew 6:25 (NIV)

Prayer. Thank you Lord, for caring for me in so many ways.

166

How fortunate (lucky) we are to have numbers in our lives. Of course, without numbers, we would not be able to count musical notes, the days of the week, months of the year, or even the years of history, money, people, account balances, the length of our lives, time, area, volume, and mass. When you start to think about numbers, you realize that they are a very big part of our existence.

I remember trying to learn historical dates at school, interestingly enough, while I can remember the process, I cannot remember the actual dates of historic events. These events are also dated from a particular point in history when we started counting the years. This was the birth of Jesus, the turning point in history which gives us BC and AD appendices to a date. Teachers would be out of work without numbers.

Eventually, there is going to be a place where numbers will not rule our lives because we will be living in a different dimension called eternity.

"And there shall be no night there; and they need no candle, neither light of the sun; for the Lord God giveth them light: and they shall reign for ever and ever." Revelation 22:5.

<u>**Prayer:**</u> Lord, I thank you that when we get to Heaven, we will never have to count anything ever again.

🍷 167

Today my lunch is Vietnamese rice paper rolls. I have made an effort to make them so they can be tried out at an organizational meeting today. In July, we will be holding a function in support of the Bible Society. This year their project is Vietnam, Cambodia, and Laos. This is one of their recipes. While I have still had to modify it to accommodate my food issues, I am looking forward to seeing what they will taste like.

The Bible Society has been carrying out the great commission for so many years.

"Go you, therefore, and teach all nations, baptizing them in the name of the Father, and of the Son, and of the Holy Spirit:" Matthew 28:19.

It is a great example to the rest of us. No, I'm not suggesting that we all start translation work, but we can support them in prayer, even if we are unable to support them financially. It only takes a minute of our time to ask God to bless these organizations and ask the Holy Spirit to work in the lives of those that they are working with.

"How then shall they call on him in whom they have not believed? and how shall they believe in him of whom they have not heard? and how shall they hear without a preacher?" Romans 10:14.

Prayer: Lord, help me to remember to pray for all those who are carrying out your great commission.

168

We have more tomatoes than we can eat. This bush is growing so well, and producing so well, that even with the three of us here, we are not able to keep up with the abundance of fruit. It is winter time and here in my father's garden, these tomatoes are still producing fruit which would just not happen at our place. The frosts would put paid to any garden producing where we are.

So many times, we are reminded that life is just not the same for all of us. The different factors that we need to deal with, such as weather, culture, lifestyle, and our backgrounds, means that we will all produce a different crop for the Lord.

That is one of the hidden truths I found in the parable of the soils or sower **(Matthew 13)**. It doesn't matter where the seed falls, it will do some good to someone, even if it is not the person that it appears to be at the time.

While I have been forced to rest the last couple of days, I have been able to do some extra reading, something I don't do a lot of under normal circumstances. I have been reading old copies of Guidepost magazine and again I am struck by the diversity of God, His love, care, and the unique way that He talks to all His creation.

Challenge. Remember that God gives us More love than we can handle.

169

I need two sets of glasses, one set to read with, and the other set to see the Television and the signs along the road while I am driving. Recently, I was thinking about needing a light when I am walking around at night.

Without the light, even in dim light, I find it very easy to lose my balance and bearings. For those who are physically blind, these issues must be coped with on a daily basis.

Many people today still have trouble thinking "outside the box" as we say, making them blind to new ideas and/or reality. God thinks very differently to the way we do, and, like the disciples, I have trouble see the things the way God wants me to.

"Therefore, they could not believe, because that Esaias said again, He hath blinded their eyes, and hardened their heart; that they should not see with *their* eyes, nor understand with *their* heart, and be converted, and I should heal them." John 12:39-40.

Prayer: Lord, help me not to be blinded to your ways.

♛ 170

Sometimes I feel a bit like an overloaded laundry basket. Yes, it's clean, but not folded or organised and over full. It takes work for me to think straight and keep calm in these situations. It takes a lot of relying on the power of prayer, on those constant conversations with God.

My mood is always influenced by the things that are happening around me. It's probably not the way it should be, but, I am human after all.

Some days, I work harder at this than others. I don't like being disorganised and I'm finding that as I get older, I am less efficient at juggling all the demands on my time. There are days when I would love to be able to turn back the clock and recapture that ability. It is at this point that God often prompts my memory to remind me of just how stressful my life used to be. He will always ask the question "Do you really want to be that stressed again?" and the answer is always "No".

Ecclesiastes 3:1 says: "To every *thing, there is* a season, and a time to every purpose under the heaven:"

A time for every purpose yes, but there is never a time to panic; move faster perhaps and even run, but not to panic.

Prayer: God you know what I need to get done, how much time I have available, please help me to get there one step at a time.

♛ 171

My house is full of a lot of things. Some are useful, some are useless and past their used by date, while other things are just for decoration. As I look around me and look at those things that are useless and really should be disposed of, I wonder why it takes me so long to actually carry out such a process. Is it because I am lazy, too proud, or do I just keep them for appearance's sake?

When it comes to those issues in my life that need to be disposed of, I find myself being reluctant to let them go as well. If I am to grow in Christ and become more like Him, then I must find a way to deal with these things. I must be willing to get rid of them, to let them go, and allow Christ to clean out all the things that are taking up room and crowding Him out.

It will be an ongoing progress of course, as there are always things that, while they are useful now, will become obsolete later and should be disposed of in due time. This applies not only to my house but also to my life.

> **"But what things were gain to me, those I counted loss for Christ. Yea doubtless, and I count all things *but* loss for the excellency of the knowledge of Christ Jesus my Lord: for whom I have suffered the loss of all things, and do count them *but* dung, that I may win Christ,"**
> **Philippians 3:7-8.**

Challenge: Pray that God will show you some things that you need to dispose of and ask Him to help you to do it.

🍷 172

I find it so easy to be focused on what has to be done, replaced, and paid for, that it is hard to keep thinking outside the circle of paying the monthly bills. There is a song that is titled "Money makes the world go round", well it doesn't. God makes the world go round, money makes humanity go around and around in circles.

The Bible tells us in 1 Timothy 6:10,

"For the love of money is the root of all evil: which while some coveted after, they have erred from the faith, and pierced themselves through with many sorrows."

No, we cannot live without some money in this day and age, however, if it controls our lives to the point where we ignore our family, friends and the problems of the world then we are not able to honour a God who makes the world rotate each day, season, and year.

As we celebrate the shortest/longest day of the year, let us remember that it is God who controls the world and when we allow Him to control us then we will be able to do more for Him and His world and a lot of money will not be necessary.

Prayer: Lord, I thank you that you made the world the way it is and it would not exist without your presence in it.

🍷 173

Someone, somewhere, said "every story has a beginning, middle and ending". Every person's life-story also has a beginning, middle, and end. Most life stories have what could be considered a prelude as well. The prelude is related to what has gone before you were born. The prelude to my life, is my parents and grandparents story, and the story of those that lived before me who contributed to my starting point. My story began in Mt Isa, Australia, where I was born. Now, as I am heading very fast towards the age of sixty, my story is still in its middle stages and will end on the day I die, or will it? There will, of course, be my epilogue, but most people will never know about that, well not until they reach Heaven themselves.

Just as God had a plan and story for Jeremiah, he also has a plan and story written for you and me.

"Before I formed thee in the belly I knew thee, and before thou camest forth out of the womb I sanctified thee, *and* I ordained thee a prophet unto the nations." Jeremiah 1:5

Yes, we might mess it up a bit from time to time, but Jesus still loves us, and He will wait for us to turn back to Him for help.

Prayer: Lord, help me to turn to you every day and not just when I am in trouble. Thank you for everyone who has contributed to my life-story.

174

The following story reminds me of just how God cares for each of us. Many years ago, a family member was going through cancer treatment. We visited the family often as we travelled backward and forwards to the farm. There was a time though when the treatment was making the family member sick. The doctors warned them that there were two viruses that needed to be avoided at all cost. One was the cold sore virus, and the other was the chickenpox virus.

When we arrived, we realized that one of my children had a cold sore and so we didn't stay. Two days later, another child came down with Chickenpox, starting an eight-week stint for me at home, as each child came down with this virus one after the other.

What we were all thankful for, was that cold sore. If the cold sore hadn't been visible, we would have stayed and only realized later that the other child was actually at their most contagious phase of the Chickenpox virus. This would have meant almost certain death for the cancer patient. God knew what was going to happen in the next few days, I didn't, I had no idea. In the most amazing way, he stopped us from causing more grief and stress on our extended family. Yes, I know that they were praying for the safe keeping of their loved one and God answered that prayer because He has our futures in His hands.

"And it shall come to pass, that before they call, I will answer; and while they are yet speaking, I will hear." Isaiah 65:24

Prayer: Lord, I praise you, because you can see the future and you have all our futures in your safe hands.

 # 175

I had a week once when I had a lot on my mind. I made many lists of things to do, in order to make sure that I didn't forget anything as I prepared for a trip away. This trip would cover several events, so I had to pack for some very different occasions. It seemed that no matter how many things I had to do, each day brought more visitors, and consequently, more things to do.

Then, to make things a little more difficult, I hurt my back which meant that I had to carry out my jobs very slowly. Once I hurt my back, I realized that I really had to calm down and think carefully so that I didn't waste time and energy running around and getting nowhere.

So, what was God trying to tell me? Psalm 46:10 says:

"Be still, and know that I _am_ God: I will be exalted among the heathen, I will be exalted in the earth."

Prayer: Lord, please show me what is important and what isn't.

176

There is a saying in the United Kingdom that says: "More haste, less speed" which means that the more you rush around the less you actually achieve.

There have been many times in my life when I have had a long list of things to do. I look at the list and think there is no way I am able to get through all this in the time I have. What I have found, is that I really have to take the time to go through that list, and prioritise each item. For instance, if I am traveling away, it is more important to pack my bags, than write a story. I can always write when I have arrived at my destination, even if it is almost a week later. There is also a point where I have to say that if I've left something behind or undone then I have to assume that it wasn't that important to start with.

We will always have things to do and yet, when God calls us home, there will still be things that we could have done or should have done. If we do what is most important first, then when that time comes, we will able to say, it wasn't that important then. What is the most important thing God wants us to do?

"Jesus said unto him, Thou shalt love the Lord thy God with all thy heart, and with all thy soul, and with all thy mind." Matthew 22:37

Prayer: Lord, may I always remember that to love you is more important than anything else in this world.

177

On very busy days, if I am sensible, I will get myself a cuppa and write out of a list of the things that I want to do. I should write down the things that need to be done first and then those extra things that I can do if I have any time left over.

Once the list is written, then I start doing the most important things first, and, when that job is completed, I find it useful to cross it off. I may even wait for an hour, grab another cuppa, and then cross off all the jobs that are finished. This gives me a progress report; I can see what I have achieved and it reminds me of what I still have to do. It also stops me from thinking that I still have many jobs to do.

Seeing what you have achieved is, in my book, just as important as seeing where you still have to go. This is different to looking back over your shoulder and living in the past.

In life, we will not always see what we have achieved, how many people we have encouraged or helped, but God knows that we do need that encouragement from time to time to help us to push on to the final goal.

> **"Wherefore comfort yourselves together, and edify one another, even as also ye do." 1 Thessalonians 5:11**

Prayer: Lord, help me to encourage others to keep going, even as if I feel discouraged myself.

🍷 178

On our family room wall hangs a canvas photo that was taken during one of the driest time we have experienced during our time here at Glenburnie Homestead. When I decided to get it printed, some of my children objected on the grounds that we didn't need to be constantly reminded of how bad the country looked during that spell. They felt that the memories would be too depressing. My husband, however, approved of the project because photos are a snapshot in time.

The interesting thing about past memories, is that we often remember things to be better than they were. The Israelites did this when they were standing on the outskirts of the Promised Land. When faced with the challenges ahead of them, they forgot how hard life was back in Egypt.

When we look at this photo, we are reminded of how dry things were. We also remember how God took care of us during such a tough time. When we turn our eyes from the photo to the green pastures outside, we thank God for the rain that has fallen. It also makes us aware that things could get that bad again sometime in the future. Maybe, when that time comes, we might do what Peter instructed us to do with more confidence:

"Casting all your care upon him; for he careth for you." 1 Peter 5:7.

Prayer: Lord, help me to remember, with honesty, how you cared for us through the tough times.

🏆 179

When things are going well, we are often heard to say that we are "on top of the world". If we are standing on the ground with clear air above us, we are of course "standing on top of the world". The world is round, well almost, and therefore there simply is no top or bottom. Yes, I know that the experts say the North Pole is the top and the South Pole is at the bottom, but if someone, way back when, had reversed that order; Australia would have been on the top of the world and not "the land down under". Now please don't get upset and tell me I'm talking a lot of rot. I agree.

I have to think that God inspired someone, maybe Adam even, to not only name the animals, but the major features of our world. Did Adam name the mountains, sea, lakes, rivers, creeks, and valleys? It seems to me that they were named long before the nations were created at the Tower of Babel **(Genesis 11:1-9).**

Maybe God even told Adam what they were called, just as He told Joseph to call Mary's baby Jesus, and Zechariah his son John. **(Luke 1:5-25).**

Prayer: Lord, I thank you created us along with the whole world and that we all have names. Thank you for loving us as individuals.

180

What do we generally mean when we say we are on top of the world? We are usually feeling good, excited, happy, pleased, and good about ourselves or things that are happening. Each day there are things that happen to make us feel better than average, and we tell ourselves that they put us on top of the world.

There are also things that make us feel bad, depressed, and lonely. In some cases, how we feel will be determined by how we react. Sometimes, events will determine how we feel; an accident can make us feel sick, in pain, or cause depression. Illness, grief, and exhaustion will never make us feel on top of the world. Even in the midst of these things we can still have a feeling of contentment, an acceptance that things will get better and that God is in control. This does not come easily but it comes through exercising our faith in God our Lord.

Paul learned it and was able to say:

"I am not saying this because I am in need, for I have learned to be content whatever the circumstances." Philippians 4:11 (NLT)

<u>Prayer:</u> Lord, during the bad, sad, and tough times, help me to remember you are in control and you will faithfully care for me.

181

Each morning I wake up with the curtains open in my room. Through the window, the sunlight fills my room for at least the first few hours of the day. That is, of course, unless there are clouds outside to hide the sun. I insist on keeping things like this as I like to see the view that God has provided for me. For those first few hours, though, it's hidden behind the bright light of the sun. I cannot see a thing from where I lie in bed without using my arm to shield the glare.

It doesn't matter where you wake up, there is a brand new day waiting for you. Its joys, sadnesses, frustrations, beauty, and problems, are hidden from all of us. What each day brings is an unopened package. Even when we know some of what we might expect, God can and will surprise us with unexpected joys, blessings, lessons and support.

"*It is of* the LORD'S mercies that we are not consumed, because his compassions fail not. *They are* new every morning: great *is* thy faithfulness." Lamentations 3:22-23

Prayer: Lord, help me to see your greatness in each new day.

182

When things make us sad, frustrated, or angry, we need to go to our Heavenly Father. His arms are always open ready to receive us and He will always hear us when we cry our hearts out to Him. Of course, we need to be willing to be open to Him. He is not a God that stands back and watches us from a distance, He is as close to us as the air we breathe. We should tell Him of our needs, frustrations, fears, and worries. Despite the fact that He already knows what our problems are and what our future holds, His ear is always open to His children. Just as His arms are open to accepting us when we come to Him. Matthew 11:28 says:

"Come unto me, all *ye* that labour and are heavy laden, and I will give you rest."

There are those who have shut God out but His arms are always open, no matter how long it has been since you spoke to Him last, even if you have never had a conversation with Him ever. He accepts anyone willing to go to Him and discover the wonderful things He has in store.

Prayer: Lord, I thank you for just being right there!

🍷 183

The older I get, the more stains I find on my clothes. I can no longer blame young babies for making such marks; they are my doing and mine alone. As I look at my shirts, my thoughts go to the stains on my life. There are many more stains on me than are on my clothes.

My thoughts also go to how hard these stains are going to be to get rid of. One washing machine I had was one of those new environmentally friendly ones, which seem to work by leaving the stains on the clothes instead of in the environment.

Thankfully, Jesus has dealt with the stains in my life. He died on the cross so that I can be forgiven of all my sins and they are covered by Him.

"In whom we have redemption through his blood, the forgiveness of sins, according to the riches of his grace;" Ephesians 1:7.

That doesn't mean that they don't exist and yes, some of them are as hard to deal with as the stains on my clothes.

It's a slow process that will go on for the rest of my life and, as the saying goes, please be patient with me because God isn't finished with me yet.

Prayer: Thank you, Jesus, for washing my soul clean, as white as snow.

🍷 184

A couple of paper-wasps stung me recently and as a result, I ended up being laid up for three weeks. We have had rain, and, as the weather is still warm, my grass is growing, but my fear of being stung again keeps me locked safely inside my house. I have been thinking about organising a function at my place in the last couple of days, so I really needed to get outside, mow my grass, and do some serious gardening. I ventured outside and got started. As I pushed that machine backward and forwards I kept my eyes peeled for any sign of nests that might be harbouring those nasty pests.

I also thought about how no matter how old I get I still have trouble stepping out confidently in faith. I guess that we never stop learning, no matter how old we get and I have a feeling that I might be a slower learner than most at trusting myself, and God.

"For God hath not given us the spirit of fear; but of power, and of love, and of a sound mind." 2 Timothy 1:7

Prayer: Lord, help me to have confidence in you.

185

We all have problems. No matter who we are, where we live, or how much we earn, we will have issues. Everyone deals with them differently, some people struggle to cope, others seem to laugh at them and move on. Yet, we must all try and do something positive about the problem. One year we had a plague of paper wasps, and, if I got bitten, which I did, I would find myself unable to do much for weeks. So, I set about making some traps for these horrible little monsters. They were not effective, but I am thankful for the protection that I experienced while I was doing what needed to be done in the garden that year.

No matter how old I get, I will continue to come face to face with problems, and stepping out in faith will sometimes be the only way to deal with them. This is something that, even at my age, I have trouble doing. This is despite that fact that God has proved to be faithful so many times before. I am a slow learner.

I think of Peter and how he was very keen to walk on the water in the same way that Jesus was doing. I don't have that same sense of adventure.

What I can learn from this event, though, is to keep my eyes on Jesus and never look down.

"And he said, Come. And when Peter was come down out of the ship, he walked on the water, to go to Jesus." Matthew 14:29.

Prayer: Lord, help me to keep my eyes on you when you ask me to move out into the rough waters of life.

186

I have a number of rose bushes, and each time I've looked out my kitchen window today, this rose has been right there, looking perfect in the sunshine.

Pink carries with it the connotation of grace and elegance, as well as sweetness and poetic romance. Dark pink roses are symbolic of gratitude and appreciation, and are a traditional way to say thanks. Light pink roses are associated with gentleness and admiration, and can also be used as an expression of sympathy. It is easy to be thankful when things look this good. It is a much harder thing to do when things are not going so well, and yet, we are told in the Bible to be thankful for all the things that happen to us. The older I get, the more I realize that God will use everything, good and bad, to make me a better person and that really is something to be thankful for.

"Giving thanks always for all things unto God and the Father in the name of our Lord Jesus Christ;" Ephesians 5:20.

Prayer: Lord, I thank you for making me a better person, help me to remember that, when things are not so good.

187

As I watch the television news about the storms today in Sydney, I remember a story that my mother told me about waking up in the middle of the night during a storm. She was frightened, but her father was there, standing beside her bed. She jumped into his arms and he was able to cuddle her and calm her down.

As I turned this story over in my mind, it occurred to me that the reason that he was already there may have been because the noise of the storm had woken him and invoked memories of the war. So, feeling a little disturbed himself, he was aware of the fears that his child might experience.

This story also reminds me of another father who is always there waiting for us to come to Him for comfort when we are afraid. His disciples were very afraid during a bad storm on the Sea of Galilee, and yet, Jesus walked out to be with them and comfort them;

"And when the disciples saw him walking on the sea, they were troubled, saying, It is a spirit, and they cried out for fear. But straightway Jesus spake unto them, saying, Be of good cheer; it is I; be not afraid."
Matthew 14:26-27.

Prayer: Lord, I thank you that your arms are always open to us to jump into during the storms of life.

188

There are four seasons in a year and, while it might be summer here in the southern hemisphere, it is winter in the northern hemisphere. I think about our men who went to war from Australia, leaving our shores in one season and arriving in the opposite season when they disembarked from the ships.

What a shock it would have been for them? Here in Australia, they would have been used to the hot dry climate and when they arrived in England, they would have found that the cold was nothing like we have here. Even though some of them would still have had family members living there, they would have been staggered.

No matter where we living on this planet, when we go to our eternal home, Heaven, or hell, we are going to be flabbergasted at what we see. It will a much greater surprise than what we experience when we move from the different hemispheres here on earth.

"And these shall go away into everlasting punishment: but the righteous into life eternal." Matthew 25:46.

Prayer: I thank you, Father, for not revealing everything to us just yet.

♈ 189

What did our soldiers in World War One snack on? From what I have been told, Beef Jerky was something that was common. My son has decided that he likes this snack which has, no doubt, been improved and certainly the packaging has improved also.

I'm sure that those soldiers would be surprised that this is a snack that is appreciated by the younger generations. I know from personal experience, that when you have no choice about what you have to eat, and it is the only food available for an extended period of time, you get to the stage where you really can't look at it again. After all, facing that particular food again will bring back memories of when you had no choice but to eat it. Our soldiers would not be able to associate good memories with this snack.

Snacks are meant to be something you eat in order to get to the next meal but many of these men had to survive on these snacks alone.

We need spiritual snacks as well. These often take the form of short readings about other's experiences with God. They are not meant to replace our daily study of God's word or prayer time but they will encourage us between these important times.

"But exhort one another daily, while it is called Today; lest any of you be hardened through the deceitfulness of sin." Hebrews 3:13

Prayer: Lord, let me be encouraged and an encouragement to others.

190

As adults, we know there are many things that we have no choice about doing. This is something that is impossible for young children to understand. It often comes as a shock to young adults as they realize that there are certain things that just have to be done, regardless as to how you feel about it.

Many young soldiers were given no choice about going to war, but they were adult enough to step up to the plate and did what had to be done for the loved ones at home and all future generations. As we remember our soldiers who fought for our freedoms, I have to ask myself, would I have the courage and determination that all those people showed?

There, of course, is one other person who showed great courage and determination. Jesus Christ, as he set out to Jerusalem, knowing that He would die on the cross. He went willingly, so that we could have freedom from sin and eternal life in Heaven. He had a choice and He made it for us.

"Looking unto Jesus the author and finisher of *our* faith; who for the joy that was set before him endured the cross, despising the shame, and is set down at the right hand of the throne of God." Hebrews 12:2

Prayer: Lord I thank you that you loved us all enough to set us free from sin.

🍷 191

Blue is the colour of the sky and sea. It is often associated with depth and stability. It symbolizes trust, loyalty, wisdom, confidence, intelligence, faith, truth, and heaven. Blue is considered beneficial to the mind and body. Considering there is so much blue in our world, created by God, it does not surprise me.

As a result, I wonder if this is why so many companies choose blue as their base colour for their offices or fittings. They are trying to send an unconscious message to all their clients that their company embraces all of the associated meanings. Having not carried out any research of my own, I have to wonder if businesses that involve higher risk might be more likely to employ blue colouring in their environment. How wonderful is it that God gave us plenty of blue to look at and made our personalities react to that precise colour in that specific way to help us relax?

"Nevertheless, the foundation of God standeth sure, having this seal, The Lord knoweth them that are his. And, let everyone that nameth the name of Christ depart from iniquity." 2 Timothy 2:19

<u>**Prayer:**</u> I thank you, Lord Jesus, that I can relax in you because you know me and my future.

🍷 192

When we travel to Sydney by train, I have noticed that the interior décor is generally blue. Thinking about other photos of the interiors of other trains, I realized that this is fairly common. So my logic is telling me that, since trains are high-speed machines that are traveling on some fairly narrow tracks, swaying from side to side, it would be easy for people to be concerned about how safe they are. Is there a perception by the designers of these machines that, by making the interior largely blue, people will unconsciously be more relaxed and therefore more confident that they will reach their destination safely? Blue is a colour used to help people relax.

Regardless of the designer's thinking, it is still easy to be afraid of the danger that travellers would be in if anything was to go wrong. Yet, no matter what we do each day, there is an element of risk. Driving on the roads can, and does, present a danger. Storms, both thunder, and snow, can cause major damage to roads, power lines, and houses.

If we are not careful, we can find ourselves looking for danger all the time. Yes, this world is only temporary, yet, God made this world for us to live in, enjoy, and travel through to the next one. The best way to enjoy this world is to remember who made it, keeps it going, and who will create the next one.

"And wisdom and knowledge shall be the stability of thy times, *and* strength of salvation: the fear of the LORD *is* his treasure." Isaiah 33:6

Prayer: Lord I thank you for being in control of my world.

🏆 193

As the rains fell, our paddocks were transformed from being boring brown, to bright green, and covered in feed. It didn't happen overnight, but it felt a bit like it. It happened because my husband had put a lot of money and hard work in before the rains came. Of course, without the rain, no transformation would have happened.

The truth is that real transformations can happen but they do not happen overnight and not without a lot of hard work. When we come to Christ to be saved and transformed, we start out on a long, hard and difficult journey. This journey will take a lifetime.

"And be not conformed to this world: but be ye transformed by the renewing of your mind, that ye may prove what *is* that good, and acceptable, and perfect, will of God." Romans 12:2.

Prayer: Lord, please transform my life into something acceptable to you, no matter how long it takes.

🍷 194

I was thinking about transformations after I woke from my first dream one night. Oh, the magic of dreams can be so amazing! In a dream, people who have died are suddenly alive and well, bad relationships no longer exist, and our world can be transformed into something that is perfect. However, we all have to wake up and face the real world. We remember those loved ones have died, the bad relationship is still not right, and our world is the same as it was the night before, if not a little more pitiful.

There will be only one instant transformation. That will be when we go home to be with our Heavenly Father. In an instant, my broken body will be transformed into a new body. I will be in a new world, a perfect world that is beyond my imagination and it will no longer be a dream.

"In a moment, in the twinkling of an eye, at the last trump: for the trumpet shall sound, and the dead shall be raised incorruptible, and we shall be changed." 1 Corinthians 15:52

Prayer: Lord, thank you for promising us all a better world if we are willing to let you be Lord of our lives.

🍷 195

I was in an accident; I was fortunate enough to come out with only one purple bruise. It won't last forever, except for the photographic record of it. It will heal, fade, and soon disappear, and before long I won't even remember it was there.

When we meet our creator, He will have a book, a written record, not a photographic one (or will it be?), of our lives here on earth which will be opened. We will remember all those things which we did, didn't do, and should have done. It will hold our memories, our good and bad ones, and the things we neglected.

"He who overcomes will thus be clothed in white garments, and I will not erase his name from the book of life, and I will confess his name before My Father and before His angels." Revelation 3:5 (NAS).

Sadly, not everyone will have that privilege.

"And if anyone's name was not found written in the book of life, he was thrown into the lake of fire." Revelation 20:15 (NAS).

However, once we have passed judgment, through the blood of Christ, the things of this world will fade from our memories. Our new eternal world will be so much better that we will have no evidence that it even existed in the first place.

"For, behold, I create new heavens and a new earth: and the former shall not be remembered, nor come into mind." Isaiah 65:17.

Prayer: Lord, our lives here on earth have a lot of pain that has to be dealt with, just like a bruise can be painful, but what a wonderful thing to look forward to; a pain-free world in Heaven.

196

For some weeks, a friend and I tried to get together for a cuppa. Each time we set a date, things went wrong, either she got sick, or I did.

So, finally, things worked out, but neither of us was planning on going to town. I only went to town because I decided that I wanted some craft supplies. When I was getting in the car, I remembered that I had some old medical supplies that needed to be taken to our Chemist. They had only been in the car for a week! As I walked into the Chemist, my friend was there talking, but I didn't interrupt them. Walking out, I commented to God that if we were to have that cuppa today, than it would be up to Him to arrange it.

As I walked back past the Chemist from another store, I almost expected to meet them walking out the door but no, there was no sign of my friend. I crossed the street and was getting into my car when my friend emerged from the shop. I watched to see where she was going and soon realized that I had parked my car right next to hers. I waited and we had that cuppa.

"The preparations of the heart in man, and the answer of the tongue *is* **from the LORD" Proverbs 16:1.**

Prayer: Lord, I thank you that when you arrange things you do a much better job than we do.

🍷 197

I had lost my sparkle and yet I really wasn't aware that it was gone. The process happened over such a long period of time that I began to feel that dull was normal. As I recover from the operations that more or less saved my life, I thank God for the right doctors, in the right place, at the right time. What a wonderful God we have.

Yet, I wonder if this is a process that happens on a spiritual level as well. Things slip slowly, and we don't notice just how our spark for God was dulled, until He pulls us up and shows us that we need to step back into His light and care.

Like the five virgins, (Matthew 25) we don't intend to let the candles go out, we just don't realize that things had got that bad.

Our loving God is always willing and able to assist us in bringing back the sparkle in our lives so that we will be able to:

"Let your light so shine before men, that they may see your good works, and glorify your Father which is in heaven." Matthew 5:16

Prayer: Lord, help me to know when my light is giving, and show me how to always shine brightly for you.

198

My calendar has many squares on it. There are small notes to remind me when we will be having a public holiday. The calendar hangs on the wall, giving an air of expectation about the month ahead. There is room to note which appointments I will need to attend, functions that I will be involved with, or other special occasions that need to be remembered.

There will be the dull, ordinary, unspectacular things that come with everyday life. Things like submitting paperwork, meetings, reporting dates, or deadlines that need to be met.

What sorts of things would I like to see noted on that calendar? Things that I find interesting, speaking engagements, book signings, things that indicate that dreams are being fulfilled, such as an overseas trip, these are things that I would like to see written all over the calendar. Realistically though, it will be the ordinary things in life that will need to be noted and completed.

I suspect that if it was filled to the max with dreams, those dreams would lose their shine and glitter. They would become ordinary things.

So, I look forward to seeing what things, both exciting, and ordinary, are put in the blank squares. What I do need to remember though, is that no matter what jobs are listed, I need to do them wholeheartedly and with all my might so that I can honour God by how I do what needs to be done.

**"And whatsoever ye do, do *it* heartily, as to the Lord, and not unto men;"
Colossians 3:23**

Challenge: To look forward no matter what is in store.

199

For breakfast I usually have a banana, walnuts, yoghurt and cups of tea. Breakfast is, as I was reminded recently, the most important meal of the day. There is a breakfast cereal advertisement on TV for Weetbix, which asks how you do your breakfast. As I was putting my meal together, I thought about our spiritual breakfast, how it might also be considered the most important spiritual meal of the day.

So I'm going to ask you, "How do you do your spiritual breakfast?" Does your Bible reading give you a boost of spiritual energy just like a banana? Do you write something down so it stays with you longer, like walnuts? Do you yearn for God to show you some new thought or idea to increase your spiritual health? Do you drink cups of thankfulness to pick you up?

Maybe you only have time for toast, trusting God to walk with you, after you enjoyed fellowship with Him the night before? Maybe you eat prayerful porridge for breakfast or cheerful Cornflakes to see you through to morning tea. Do you eat your breakfast slowly, enjoying each mouthful or do you eat it on the run? Maybe you skip breakfast altogether?

"Study to shew thyself approved unto God, a workman that needeth not to be ashamed, rightly dividing the word of truth." 2 Timothy 2:15.

Challenge: Don't forget to feed on God's word each day.

200

I was thinking about how some people have growth charts to record how tall their children have grown over the last year or so. They often measure them on their birthday every year. It was something we did not have when we were kids, because we didn't own the houses that we lived in. I do not remember even having such a growth chart in the other two houses that we own either. I guess I felt, deep down, that we were only passing through these two places. Once we moved to the farm, I declared that my next move would happen in my "pine box". It had been such an undertaking that I really did not, and still do not, want to do it again.

When I get to Heaven, I will be able to stay in the same house forever. Oh, what a wonderful thought that is. I won't even have to pack my worldly goods up to make the move to Heaven. I cannot take anything with me when I move from this world to the next. It is just as well, as I would have no idea what to take with me.

"For we *are* strangers before thee, and sojourners, as *were* all our fathers: our days on the earth *are* as a shadow, and *there is* none abiding." 1 Chronicles 29:15

Prayer: Lord, I am still only passing through this world, please help me to do what I can with what you have given me.

201

While we do not need to be pedantic about what we do for our spiritual growth, we do need to stay close to God in a way that suits our lifestyles, needs, and circumstances. If I was to have what is considered a regular breakfast, I would be sick for days and so it is with all Christians, we need to gain our spiritual food in a way that will bring us closer to God, not drive us away.

This is why man-made rules and regulations do not always work. We all come from different backgrounds and social environments. One thing is certain in my mind, and that is that God made us all different. The only things that fit every person everywhere are the Love of God and how He reaches down to us as individuals.

I'm not saying that we don't need frameworks to work within, but we do need enough compassion to realize that not everyone will be comfortable with what we decide is right.

"For God so loved the world, that he gave his only begotten Son, that whosoever believeth in him should not perish, but have everlasting life." John 3:16

Prayer: Lord, I thank you for the love that you have for me and for all of mankind.

🍷 202

We have a lawnmower that is well over twenty years old. It is showing signs of its age. It's rough and ready and it starts with rope. It has trouble getting started some mornings, particularly after it's been on holidays due to wet weather, or it has been waiting for the grass to grow. On these occasions, I have to enlist the help of "Aerostart" and either my husband, or son's muscles. When it goes, it does a very good job!

This lawnmower reminds me of myself some days. I'm a bit rough and ready and battered even. I have trouble getting started more mornings than I care to admit. I'm showing quite a few scars and wrinkles of life. The most wonderful thing is, that like my mower, I am still useful to God. No, we don't need a rope to get us started but let's rest in Him and start anyway.

"Not slothful in business; fervent in spirit; serving the Lord; Rejoicing in hope; patient in tribulation; continuing instant in prayer;" Romans 12:11-12

Prayer: Thank you, Lord, for making me useful, no matter what state I find myself in.

203

Even if I was completely broken physically (bedridden), I would be able to lie there and pray all day, and God could use that. He heard the prayers of a bedridden lady in England in 1872, and sent a revival through the preaching of D L Moody (Christian Preachers, Nigel Clifford p 291). I'm not bedridden however, and yes, if you get me fired up, I can still move a mountain of work. Mind you – afterward, I need to rest to get over it.

There are three things to remember about what we do for the Lord:
1. It's what He wants us to do;
2. That we do it with all our heart soul and mind and
3. It's for His glory, not ours.
We are instructed to:

"Rest in the LORD, and wait patiently for him: fret not thyself because of him who prospereth in his way, because of the man who bringeth wicked devices to pass." Psalm 37:7

Prayer: Even as a completely broken person, I know that you love me and can use me.

204

One morning I had to face a sink full of dirty dishes. I'd had a busy day or two, and I just could not face the dishes the night before. As the mountain of dishes dissolved, my thoughts turned to how quickly things are done when we stop messing around and just start the job that is in front of us.

In the past, I have asked my children to do something and their cry has been "but that's just too big for me to do!" Yet the job has always been accomplished when they have tackled it, one toy, one article of clothing, or one piece of rubbish at a time.

I was discussing a project with someone recently, and they commented that they would only be able to carry it out if everything fell into place. My response was that things don't work like that. The only way to make it happen is to put things in place so that they could do what they wanted. What do they say, a journey of a thousand miles starts with one step but if we don't take a step we will be forever at the starting line? Of course, we must not plan without asking God to guide us along the way.

**"In all thy ways acknowledge him, and he shall direct thy paths."
Proverbs 3:6**

Prayer: Please direct not only my paths, but my planning as well.

205

Often, as I work my way through the mountain of dirty dishes that is a result of eating meals, I pray. I might pray for a young family who are facing grief again, for friends who I know are going through tough times, or for the meeting I have coming up. I might pray that God would give me a sense of humour when I have to face some "big people" in my life. I thank God for the other authors and friends who have encouraged me as I learn all about being an author. I also thank Him for the lack of panic that I sometimes feel, when I am feeling muddled headed and unmotivated.

As I stand at the sink, I talk to God, not aloud or in a formal way, but as a friend. I try also to listen to what He might say to me, quietly through my thoughts. There has been many a time, while I have been standing at the sink thinking about friends, that I have felt the need to give them a call. When I have called, I have tried to encourage them and tell them that I have been thinking about them and praying.

No, I have never had the experience of ringing someone and being a major answer to their prayers, but I know that I have felt better just talking to them.

> "Praying always with all prayer and supplication in the Spirit, and watching thereunto with all perseverance and supplication for all saints;"
> Ephesians 6:18

Prayer: Remember all my friends and please keep them safe.

206

Most of my days start with a cup of tea. I am often woken by my husband with my first cup of the day, even if he is going off to work. There are varying opinions on how good or bad this drink is for us, but I know that I feel better after having one. Most people who know me have a good stock on hand for when I come to visit.

Another thing that I should do first thing in the morning is delve into the word of God, or at least have a conversation with Him to get my day off to a good start.

When I do; He teaches me about His desires for me,

> "Teach me thy way, O LORD; I will walk in thy truth: unite my heart to fear thy name." Psalm 86:11

Enlightens me about where He would like me to go, and what He would like me to do

> "Thy word *is* a lamp unto my feet, and a light unto my path." Psalm 119:105,

Assures me of my salvation in Christ

"Truly, truly, I say to you, whoever hears my word and believes him who sent me has eternal life. He does not come into judgment, but has passed from death to life." John 5:24 (ESV).

So, when you start your day with a cup of T.E.A. just remember that God would like to join you and Teach, Enlighten and Assure you as well.

Prayer: Thank you for all the ways that you use to teach me.

🍷 207

If we look at the word "Still", we realise we can use so many other words in its place, such as motionless, immobile, unmoving, tranquil, silent, quiet, stagnant, and static, which could be related to lifelessness. As I listened to the night sounds during a recent storm, I was surprised that life outside had become very still. There were no birds singing, no chooks crowing and even the dogs were quiet. It had a very eerie feel to it, which was quite uncomfortable.

Yet, there have been other times when I have woken up first thing in the morning to the same stillness and quietness, and not felt any discomfort at all. A stark contrast to the mornings when the chooks have been noisy and the dogs have been barking. On these mornings, it is very hard to lie quietly and talk to God, like the animals, I want to get up and get moving.

"Be still, and know that I _am_ God: I will be exalted among the heathen, I will be exalted in the earth." Psalm 46:10

Prayer: Lord, let me remember to take the time to be still and listen to you, even if your creation is up and about.

208

If we then look at the word "life", we get lifetime, lifespan, lifecycle, existence, and being.

Life is about moving. Some of us move forward, others move round and round in circles, and still others will move backward, but we all move. Some of us slowly, others are fast movers, and some people will move at a steady pace.

Some people will struggle, while others will breeze through life. No matter how we get through life, we will all end up having to give an account of how faithfully we have made our way through it. It is only as we move through life in the way that God wants us to, and use the strength and power given to us by His son, Jesus Christ, that we will be able to say with Paul.

"I have fought a good fight, I have finished *my* course, I have kept the faith:" 2 Timothy 4:7.

Prayer: Lord, I thank you for the strength, power, and love that you give.

209

The phase "while there is still life, there is hope" is often said when people are very ill or living life in a manner that is not acceptable to most of us.

However, "while there is still life, there is hope", is a great thought to hang on to when we think things are always going wrong, and we don't seem to be able to move forward. While people are still hanging on to their life here on earth, there is time for them to make the right choices, which will affect their eternal life. That eternal life will go on forever but it is determined by how we live our lives here and now.

When things look bleak, let us look to the power of God and ask Him where we should be going because that is where our hope lies.

> "Our soul has waited for Yahweh.
> He is our help and our shield.
> For our heart rejoices in him,
> because we have trusted in his holy name.
> Let your loving kindness be on us, Yahweh,
> since we have hoped in you." Psalm 33:20-22.

Prayer: Lord, you are my rock and my salvation, I thank you for always being there for me.

🍷 210

It's late afternoon and the sun is shining in through my window. As I looked at the window, I noticed just how dirty it was. I realized that the dirt was more noticeable because the sun was behind it.

It occurred to me that our lives are like my window. Dirty with sin. Yet it takes Jesus, the Son of God, and the Holy Spirit to shine on it, for us to see it. I had to smile at the differences between the effects of the Sun on my window and God's Son on my life. That sun shining through my window wasn't going to be able to clean it. It would only bake that dirt on more and make it harder to clean off. While Jesus, the Son of God, will clean my life of dirt and shame, if I would only ask Him.

> "Come now, and let us reason together, saith the LORD: though your sins be as scarlet, they shall be as white as snow; though they be red like crimson, they shall be as wool." Isaiah 1:18.

Prayer: Lord, Jesus please clean my life so that others will be able to see you through me.

211

During the winter, the sun streams through our large, loungeroom windows. The room glows with a brightness that only the sun could create. It's a very warm place to sit and I enjoy it immensely.

One day, I noticed that the windows were dirty. If I had drawn the curtains against the cold winter weather, I would have also been able to hide them. If I had, of course, the room would have been plunged into a dreary darkness.

Yes, I can draw the curtains on my life and ignore the sin that is there. I can cover it up with explanations of "I'm human", "I'm not perfect" or "I'm just busy". It doesn't matter how I cover sin up, God can always see it. Eventually, God is going to pull those curtains back and He is going to say, "Look, child, I want to help you see a better way, a nicer room, a clearer, brighter view of the world".

"Neither is there any creature that is not manifest in his sight: but all things *are* naked and opened unto the eyes of him with whom we have to do." Hebrews 4:13

Prayer: I know that you see everything that I do and think, forgive me of my sins.

212

I have always suffered from low-level depression. Over the years, God has shown me that certain mineral deficiencies have not helped the situation, and that by correcting those I have been able to control the issue. There have been some dark days when I knew that I had taken care of my body enough to know that it has not been a deficiency of some mineral or vitamin. It was not about a lack of spiritual faith either. It is most likely about God making me more aware of how others might feel, and trying to understand that God wants me to be able to relate to them in a very small way. I can never say that have walked in their shoes, so I can never fully understand their pain, but I can get it, that life is not fair and that some valleys can be long and seem to take forever to get through.

God walks with us. We may feel alone, but in those moments, God has to teach me that feelings can lie. It is necessary for me to put my feelings aside and remember the facts. Facts like, God loves me, He cares for me, and He has my best interests at heart.

I remember, as a child, feeling that my mother was being mean to me when in fact she knew better than I did about what the consequences of certain activities would be. Now, let's face it, God knows more than my mother ever did.

"Remember the former things of old: for I *am* God, and *there is* none else; *I am* God, and *there is* none like me," Isaiah 46:9

<u>Prayer:</u> Help me to learn how to be able to relate to others with compassion.

🍷 213

The sun is rising on yet another brand new day. Its flares spread out right across the valley. I have been thinking about how our world is made up of mountains and valleys even beneath the oceans. Some of those mountains are very high and the valleys can be very deep.

My life has always been a series of mountain experiences followed by long walks in valleys, some have been broad and wide, others have been deep and rough going.

We are taught to be afraid and ashamed of depression, stress, and sadness, but they are a part of the valleys that we have to walk through. I know there are certain types that need professional intervention in the form of medication or counselling, but I have decided that for me, today, a tough day, I am going to keep going. God loves me and has a lesson for me today.

"Yea, though I walk through the valley of the shadow of death, I will fear no evil: for thou art with me; thy rod and thy staff they comfort me."
Psalm 23:4

Prayer: Lord, I thank you that even though I cannot see you, you are always right by my side.

214

God allows us to have some mountain experiences to help us see that the world is much bigger than the valleys we walk through but they are usually short stays. For those of us who are walking in valleys of despair, sadness, or not feeling up to par, it can be hard to see those sun-flares of God's love reaching out to us. The temptation is for us to want to stay on top of the mountains and avoid the reality of our world. That reality can be very grim a lot of the time.

We are not alone in this. Peter wanted to stay on the mountain at the transfiguration (Matthew 17), so we are all in good company. Besides, how can God be glorified, if His people stayed on the mountaintops? They need to be mixing with the people down in the valleys, sharing their reality just as Jesus did Himself. If He had stayed in Heaven we would still be living under the law, not grace.

Let us all look up, see the sun shining down on us and if the clouds are covering it, let us just remember that God has not failed us, but is strengthening our faith in Him.

"He restoreth my soul: he leadeth me in the paths of righteousness for his name's sake." **Psalm 23:3**

Prayer: Lord, you left Heaven to show us how to live, help us to be faithful.

🍷 215

We have to sow our paddocks on faith. One year my husband went out, purchased "Super" and "Super Dan" seed, and planting got underway.

"Super" is the fertilizer that will help the seeds to get a good start in life. "Super Dan" is the name of the grass that will, if all things go well, give us enough feed for our stock or make hay. It would be easy to think that, with all this super stuff, we will end up with a super amount of feed. However, it will be the ordinary things such as sunshine and rain that will ensure a bumper crop.

So it is with us. It doesn't matter what sort of start you have in life. You may be born with the best privileges and advantages that society can offer, but you won't necessarily make a success of your life. It is the ordinary things, love, care, understanding, and good choices that enable people to make a good contribution to our society.

Once you have made the most of the resources around you, you can only step out in faith and move forward one step at a time. The results will then be up to God, and He will work, even if we don't get the results that we would like. We had no guarantees that this crop was going to be successful, but we carried on in a sensible manner. We still trust God to look after the future.

"Trust in the LORD with all thine heart, and lean not unto thine own understanding." Proverbs 3:5.

<u>*Prayer:*</u> Lord, I thank you for always looking after us.

🍷 216

There are a great number of Superannuation funds in Australia and they do perform at differing rates of success. What reserves people have available when they retire, will depend on just how well these funds perform.

Staff members are also able to sacrifice part of their salaries to add to these funds. It is a means of storing up funds against a future need.

While it is a sensible thing to do in order to try and prevent workers being dependent on Government pensions, it is still a material good that can be eroded by the fall of stock markets and the bad performance of investments.

Matthew 6:19-21 warns us to;

"Lay not up for yourselves treasures upon earth, where moth and rust doth corrupt, and where thieves break through and steal: But lay up for yourselves treasures in heaven, where neither moth nor rust doth corrupt, and where thieves do not break through nor steal: For where your treasure is, there will your heart be also."

That is not saying to be silly when it comes to business practices but it is telling us to remember that, in the end, all things on earth will rot away and we are not able to take anything into eternity with us. We cannot force people to follow Jesus, but if we share the gospel, and carry out acts of kindness that help others make that choice, then we are laying up treasure in Heaven.

Prayer: Lord, show where I can lay up treasure in Heaven by bringing people to my door so that I might speak to them about you.

217

How sweet are childhood memories? They were times when most of us enjoyed very few responsibilities. I am grateful for such a start in life.

Those good memories are a place I go to when I am feeling tired, stressed, and frustrated with adulthood. When late night phone calls give you cause for concern, illness and pain keep you awake into the early hours of the morning, or you need a good place go to in order to distract yourself. My childhood memories are that place for me.

Do you remember thinking that adults could do as the pleased? I do! Even my children accused me of this privilege. Adult life has a habit of handing you a great number of responsibilities, all of which we are very unaware of as children. I am sure we all have days when all these things weigh heavy on us and we would love to be children again.

"When I was a child, I spake as a child, I understood as a child, I thought as a child: but when I became a man, I put away childish things." 1 Corinthians 13:11

When we have one of those days, it seems hard to understand what God would like us to do. 1 Corinthians 13:12 seems very relevant;

"For now we see through a glass, darkly; but then face to face: now I know in part; but then shall I know even as also I am known."

Prayer: Thank you, Lord, that one day I will see clearly what sweet plans God has for me.

♈ 218

When we say, "Thank You", we are indicating an attitude of thankfulness. This is easy enough when things are going well, but I also find personally, that it is still very easy to forget to say thank you. I get so caught up with how good things are that I just forget to say it.

When things are not going so well, thankfulness as an attitude is still harder to find. We can get so bogged down trying to figure out how to fix the situation, or depressed that we cannot see anything to say thank you for. It is there, even if it is only one small thing, but it is hard to see.

"In everything give thanks: for this is the will of God in Christ Jesus concerning you." 1 Thessalonians 5:18

Prayer: Lord, even when I cannot see something to be thankful for, help me to remember to say thank you anyway.

219

Just the act of saying thank you to someone can make them feel so much better about themselves. Even if someone is behaving badly, I try to find something to say thank you to them for and make them feel better.

I remember a time when I did just that to a young person who had been caught stealing from us. I found something good that they had done, thanked them for it, and I am sure that made the young person feel a little better about themselves.

We have found and purchased a kitchen unit that I had been trying to find for about two years. Did I thank God for making me wait while I was actually waiting? Not really. I would talk to God and say "I know you have a solution" but I am not sure that is the same thing.

"In everything give thanks: for this is the will of God in Christ Jesus concerning you." I Thessalonians 5:18.

Prayer: Lord, please forgive my lack of thankfulness.

220

The year 2014 was a challenging year for me, which revolved around one event, the accident that my parents were involved in and which took the life of my mother. However, I would not change anything about that year. I have learned a lot of new things; things about resting in, waiting on, listening to, and leaning on the Lord God. I have seen so many miracles.

When the police posted their report about my parents on the internet, there was not one person who was unkind in their remarks, which is extraordinary.

Earlier in the year, I had a feeling of panic which forced me to finish the manuscript for my second book, and by listening to God (because I believe that this feeling came from Him), I submitted my last story on the day before that momentous accident, which I consider to be extraordinary.

The cancelling of my first overseas trip because there were not sufficient numbers to make up the tour, while a mystery, was extraordinary, because that tour would have started just a couple of weeks after mum's death.

My health had played up during the middle of the year, which, while being frustrating, meant that I was unable to make some commitments that I would not have been able to fulfil the week of the accident.

"And do not seek what you will eat and what you will drink, and do not keep worrying. For all these things the nations of the world eagerly seek, but your Father knows that you need these things." Luke 12:29-30 (NAS).

Prayer: Thank you, Lord, for knowing what I need even before I do.

🍷 221

There was a time when I refused be bullied by an ex-husband of one of my children. He had decided that I was not allowed to work with my daughter. We needed the money; she needed the help, and so I accepted the work, but it meant that he wasn't told about it.

I stayed with a friend and we were very careful about answering and making calls on the phone. However, one Sunday morning I went to church and, after church, I was invited to stay and take part in a Bible Study group. I nearly declined but then thought no, why not, I'll stay. Afterward, I arrived back at my friend's place to find out that I had missed two phone calls because I had my phone on silent . The first one was to tell me that son-in-law had turned up at her place and to stay away until she rang me back, the other was to say it was safe to come home. If God had not inspired me to stay at the church, my daughter would have had a lot of stress to deal with.

There are times when we do have to take a stand against evil and when we do God is there to protect and hide us.

"He shall cover thee with his feathers, and under his wings shalt thou trust: his truth *shall be thy* shield and buckler." Psalm 91:4

Prayer: Lord, I thank you for all the times that you have protected me.

222

I received a Jacaranda tree for my birthday one year. We thought that the one that had been planted previously had died, so, we decided to plant my birthday tree in the same place. We arrived at the spot only to find that it wasn't dead, there were new leaves hidden in amongst the weeds surrounding it.

There are many times in our lives when it can seem to be just like that tree, there was new growth, there was life, there was progress, but it was so hard to find it because a lot of tough stuff surrounded it.

God is in the midst of all that happens, good, bad, beautiful, and ugly, and out of it all, He will be faithful. He will help us to grow. No one else might be able to see it but He can, and He will water and feed up so that one day our heads to be higher than the weeds and we will see His light.

"Though I walk in the midst of trouble, thou wilt revive me: thou shalt stretch forth thine hand against the wrath of mine enemies, and thy right hand shall save me." Psalm 138:7

Prayer: Lord, I thank you that you help me to grow, even when I cannot see anything but trouble.

223

One of the things that I needed to do for my father on a certain visit was to repair a pair of trousers. When I unpicked all the stitching, there was a large gap that appeared. Now I haven't kept my sewing skills up to date as I have a very talented daughter who I often delegate my sewing jobs to. Why should I struggle with these things when she can do them so much faster and better than I can? So, it was with a little trepidation that I started this project. About half way through this process, I looked at my progress and wondered if I would be able to complete it to a satisfactory level. I realized that if wasn't careful, I could easily have developed a negative mind space about my abilities to complete the job. I just needed to take it slowly and carefully, measuring before cutting.

It could also happen with other duties and projects that I undertake in life. If I try to rush it and do it in my own strength, I will mess it up. I need to make sure that God is in the planning stages and that He will assist me along the way but I can only expect that if I am doing what He wants in the first place.

"The heart of man plans his way, but the Lord establishes his steps." Proverbs 16:9 (ESV).

<u>**Prayer:**</u> Lord, help me to reduce the number of negative thoughts and focus on you instead.

224

My bedroom is my closet.

"But thou, when thou prayest, enter into thy closet, and when thou hast shut thy door, pray to thy Father which is in secret; and thy Father which seeth in secret shall reward thee openly." Matthew 6:6.

This is where I can be quiet; our house is still very noisy even though the kids have left home. It is also where I write, work, and share fellowship with my friends on Facebook. It is also where I sleep. I often make phone calls in this room because it is quiet.

It is also where I talk to my Father in Heaven, first thing in the morning and last thing at night as I fall off to sleep. It has always been a place where I have been able to talk to my children and where we have had those serious discussions that need to be had. Yes, there are times when I allow the world to invade my silence. The tv has a way of doing that. Yes, in my bedroom I sleep, eat, write, talk, dream, plan, work and pray but I always try to do it all with the Lord at my side.

> "And whatsoever ye do, do *it* heartily, as to the Lord, and not unto men;
> Colossians 3:23

Prayer: Lord, thank you for listening.

225

I was thinking about how babies find so many things fascinating; things such as a piece of fluff, a scrap of paper or dirt. Why do they find these things, which make adults cringe, remarkable? It is because their world is so new.

As we grow older, as our world becomes familiar, it can lose its allure. What we find interesting will depend on what talents we have, where our interests lie, and our personalities. So many things interest people. Things like gardening, relationships between people, outer space, mechanics, medicine, the list is endless.

I remember years ago, when my husband was in the hospital on life support, being absolutely amazed by the passion and drive of the nurses and doctors. I could not even imagine why they were so interested in medicine. That dedication saved, not only my husband's life, but my father's as well after a major accident. I am very grateful for their perseverance. Life would be very dull however if we all had the same interests. Progress is a result of people having different interests and passions. We should use what talents, interests, and passions we have to make this world a better place, bringing humanity together and improving life for everyone.

"**Having then gifts differing according to the grace that is given to us,......**" **Romans 12.6.**

Prayer: Let me use my talents for you and you only.

 **226**

Several years ago, I took a part-time job as a Show Society Secretary. What I discovered about myself, and I honestly never expected this, was that I was passionate about the show movement and the opportunities that it offers farmers to educate our city cousins about where and how their food is produced. Oh, how I wish we were able to show people in towns and cities that farmers are good carers of our land and remind them that, without farmers, they would not be able to eat as well as they currently do.

A few years on, and my time with the "show movement" has ended. I still want to make sure that our city cousins know what farming is all about. How to do that is a big question that I have no answer to yet. The time there, like many other phases in our lives is over, it is now time to move on to something else. I have often discovered that one activity can be preparation for something else.

"**To everyt**_hing, there is_ **a season, and a time to every purpose under the heaven:**" **Ecclesiastes 3:1.**

Prayer: Lord, lead me to where you need me most.

227

In 2011, I started writing short stories for our Church news sheet. This eventually led to publishing my first book *Turning Water into Wine*. I continued to write. What I didn't expect, was to feel so passionate about using this type of media. An eye defect that I was born with, was discovered and fixed in my thirties. It prevented me from enjoying writing when I was at school. It also coloured my belief system about my capabilities. I honestly thought I was incapable of being able to write. Throw in the odd card and some gardening and God just amazes me.

Still, as I listen to the audio version of my book while driving, I hear those stories and I am amazed that I actually put the words together. So much so that each time I have to say "God only you could do this".

"Blessed *be* the God and Father of our Lord Jesus Christ, who hath blessed us with all spiritual blessings in heavenly *places* in Christ:"
Ephesians 1:3.

Prayer: Lord, thank you for all that you have given me.

228

I cannot drink coffee, but my children can, and so, each time I open a tin of coffee, I smell the aroma and oh, it smells so good. The trouble is, that if I were to actually drink a cup of coffee, I wouldn't feel so good.

With these thoughts came thoughts about how so many of our advertisers work on the principle of "if it feels good, do it". The hope is that people will buy whatever product they are selling, in order to make themselves feel good. Then, when that doesn't work, they will continue to buy more and more things, looking for that good feeling.

It is very common to take the easy way out. If the coffee didn't actually make me very sick, there is no way I would be able to resist the temptation to drink some. I won't reveal how many cups of coffee a day I used to drink, but it was a lot.

Resisting temptation is sometimes made easier by being afraid of the consequences. In these days of the "feel good" approach, too many people are not afraid of them and are even willing to deal with them.

Sooner or later we will have to deal with them anyway. As we read in Revelation 20:15,

"And whosoever was not found written in the book of life was cast into the lake of fire."

This isn't just about resisting temptations, of course, but also about failing to take God at His word that, if we ignore the sacrifice of Jesus, there will be consequences.

Prayer: Lord, I know that you will help me to resist the temptations that this life will throw at me.

229

We have, at times, no power connected to our house. It might be because a storm has damaged the infrastructure or the company has turned it off to do maintenance. Whatever the reason, I don't like being dependent on one commodity.

We are better off than most people are in our area. We, at least, have a wood burning stove, gravity fed water, and battery backup on our computer. Some people who live on farms don't even have water once their electricity stops because they rely on electric pumps to get water to their homes. Therefore, for some people their world almost stops with a power outage. Thinking about being very dependent on something, reminds me that we are all totally dependent on God, not only for life, but also for salvation. Without Him, all life would stop!

"The LORD is my rock and my fortress and my deliverer, My God, my rock, in whom I take refuge; My shield and the horn of my salvation, my stronghold." Psalm 18:2 (NAS).

Prayer: Lord, I thank you that I can always depend on you.

230

My granddaughter is nearly six years old and, while I could be considered biased, I can see her potential. It is raw and childlike, but then the artist is only a child. If the raw talent is nurtured, practiced, and developed, then one day I could be attending an art gallery featuring her work. This is, of course, just speculation and no one can predict what the future holds for this wonderful little girl. She will face many challenges and situations, which will all shape her destiny in one way or another.

Neither can we predict what is around the corner for our own lives. I often wonder how people can even try to predict what might happen in 100 years time. After all, we are not in control and there are so many variables, which can change any outcome. God is the only one that knows the future and He also knows the outcomes.

"If I ascend up into heaven, thou *art* there: if I make my bed in hell, behold, thou *art there.*" Psalm 139:8

And that is not speculation!

Prayer: Lord, you know what my future holds, help me not to speculate but to trust you to lead me in the right direction.

231

My granddaughter is very talented, and is willing to have a go at anything, particularly art. She reminds me of how our lives as Christians can be like her art. No matter how old we are when we come to Jesus and start our walk with Him, our faith is raw and childlike. It needs to be nurtured, practiced, and developed, so that it will grow into something beautiful for the world to see. It will be able to pass on messages of love, patience, and encouragement to those who see the growth that takes place. Yes, its growth will be determined by the challenges and situations, both good and bad, that the person has to go through, but the hand of God will always be there to guide and direct them. The big difference here is that, while I cannot see what is in my granddaughter's future, God can, and He sees all our futures.

"Neither is there any creature that is not manifest in his sight: but all things *are* naked and opened unto the eyes of him with whom we have to do." Hebrews 4:13

Prayer: Help me to encourage others so that they will grow closer to you.

♈ 232

When I clean out my cupboards, I find all sort of things that had been hidden from public view. I don't make that effort very often. Once, I found a pair of earrings that I missed, a football belonging to my now grown son, pegs, a corn fork, and a needle.

As I swept, scrubbed, washed, and sorted the mess I thought about how we hide things from public view. We can cover our fears, our anger, and disappointments from others, particularly if we are careful to present a happy and confident front when we are out and about.

However, that there is one person we cannot hide from, no matter how hard we try. God sees all our tears, fears, joys, and achievements. He sees everything, right down to those thoughts we like to keep to ourselves. Yes, you may not see everything that I do, but God does! It doesn't matter how many faults I have right now because He is working on me. He is cleaning, sweeping, and sorting me out. A process that will take as long as I live. It will be ongoing and one day, it will be complete. On that day I will go to be with Him and know that it has been worth all the hard work.

"**If I ascend up into heaven, thou *art* there: if I make my bed in hell, behold, thou *art there*." Psalm 139:8.**

<u>Prayer:</u> Lord, I am glad that you will continue to work in my life for as long as I am here on earth.

233

In our western society, there almost seems to be a fear of tradition. Maybe it is because we see them as being tight and inflexible. I remember years ago, reading a story about a young widow feeling very frustrated because the tradition of wearing black for mourning had been done away with. It wasn't that she didn't believe her husband was in heaven or that she had no hope of seeing him again, but the fact was that her life was not the same, and she wanted some way to tell people that her life was different, and that she was hurting without having to explain it in words.

As we read the Bible, we see that there were many traditions that the Jews held on to, and yes, the spirit of these events was often abused. Jesus had a bit to say about them but He also told us to observe some traditions as well. Let us be careful not to throw away all our traditions because some of them are there to remind us of the goodness of God.

"And he took bread, and gave thanks, and brake *it*, and gave unto them, saying, This is my body which is given for you: this do in remembrance of me." Luke 22:19.

<u>Prayer:</u> Lord, may I never forget your goodness to me.

234

A compost heap is made up of weeds, rubbish, and garden waste, which is mixed together and left to break down and change into a product that can then be returned to the garden to revitalize the new seedlings. They will draw on the food that the compost provides to grow stronger, healthier, and full of goodness. We cannot survive without food, we can survive even on very poor quality food if we have to, previous generations and current communities are a testimony to that, but the better the quality of our food, the better our health will be.

On a spiritual level, we can also survive on poor spiritual food. This is what happens when church leaders get off track and do not preach strictly to the word of God. One of the advantages of our current internet services is that, if we are not getting good spiritual food at home, we can hunt it down through that facility.

On a personal level, isn't it wonderful how God will take my life, something that is not really worth a lot as a sinner and transform me into something that will feed and encourage those around me!

"Wherefore comfort yourselves together, and edify one another, even as also ye do." 1 Thessalonians 5:11

<u>Prayer:</u> Oh Lord, may I be someone today that will enrich the lives of those around and not be trash that just gets in the way.

235

I treasure memories of my mother's love, care, and common sense. A picture that comes to mind is that one that was shared around the world of two princes running to their mother (Princess Diana) on the royal yacht after they had been separated because their parents had to carry out royal duties.

Work, illness, and stress drain the resources of all humans. During the bad days, we all would have loved to run into her arms for another cuddle and some "common sense" advice.

In the light of day, I realize that the reality is that she has been taken home to heaven, and I can only draw on all those conversations that we had over the years. Yes, one day I will run into her arms again, and the arms of Jesus will also be there. In the meantime, I have to rest in Him and listen to his voice.

Matthew 11:30 "Come unto me, all *ye* that labour and are heavy laden, and I will give you rest. Take my yoke upon you, and learn of me; for I am meek and lowly in heart: and ye shall find rest unto your souls. For my yoke *is* easy, and my burden is light."

<u>Prayer:</u> During bad days, it is hard to remember where our help really comes from. Lord, please help me to remember that the safest arms are yours.

236

As I looked at the clouds, I could see that some were storm clouds and others were just rain clouds. I thought about what the colours tell me, the dark colours tell me that damage could be done if those dark clouds contain heavy rain, lightning, and hail. The other clouds would be rain that would be more of a help than a hinderance. But, regardless of what those clouds produced, they were still clouds, not blue sky.

It might be a strange thought, but what followed were thoughts about how people see sin. We grade it into various levels, those really bad ones like murder, stealing, and fraud and the not so bad ones like lies, bad language, and temper. Of course, there are those that we ignore altogether, the ones where we disregard God and His goodness, His gift of Salvation and His plan for our lives. In the end, God will call sin, sin.

"Now the works of the flesh are manifest, which are *these*; Adultery, fornication, uncleanness, lasciviousness, Idolatry, witchcraft, hatred,

variance, emulations, wrath, strife, seditions, heresies, Envying, murders, drunkenness, revelling, and such like: of the which I tell you before, as I have also told *you* in time past, that they which do such things shall not inherit the kingdom of God." Galatians 5:19-21

Prayer: Lord, sin is sin, please stop me from calling it anything else.

♛ 237

"Can you get up please, Uncle Alex, I want to play chess?" This was my granddaughter's request to her uncle who works night shift and eight in the morning is just too early for him. After about an hour, he did rise to the occasion, as all good uncles do. I see this in myself. My reluctance to get out of my comfortable spiritual bed and do what God wants me to do. How easy is it to stay within my comfort zone and not step up to a new challenge? I'm not quite as good as Abram at picking up stumps and moving forward, it would seem.

"Now the LORD had said unto Abram, Get thee out of thy country, and from thy kindred, and from thy father's house, unto a land that I will shew thee:" Genesis 12:1

Prayer: God thank you for loving us enough to keep prompting us to move out of our comfort zone

♛ 238

My granddaughter had come to visit while her uncle was still living at home. He was working night shift but she wanted to play a game of pool. The thing was, she asked him to get up and play chess instead. It took me a little while to realize what she was actually asking.

I was thinking about how we, as humans, ask God for things. We ask, but years later discover that what we wanted was not what we actually asked for. It's just as well the Holy Spirit knows what I am asking for and can interpret. He also knows before we do, what we are asking, which is a very good thing indeed.

"Likewise the Spirit also helpeth our infirmities: for we know not what we should pray for as we ought: but the Spirit itself maketh intercession for us with groanings which cannot be uttered." Romans 8:26

Prayer: Lord, I praise you for knowing exactly what I want, what I need, knowing the difference, and knowing what I am really asking for.

 **239**

Stained glass windows were used in the past to help teach those who couldn't read, the truth of scripture. There are so many things these days that we can use to teach our children, the best way though, is to be a very good example in the way we live. Then they might understand more about what it means to be a Christian. We can only do this by making sure that we understand the love of God for ourselves. Then we can explain why we give gifts at Christmas time, eat Hot Cross Buns at Easter, be kind to those who hurt us, and give away unwanted goods to charity. We are remembering that God gave the human race the greatest gift of all in order to ensure that we will be able to accept the gift of Salvation and have eternal life when this life is over.

"In all things shewing thyself a pattern of good works: in doctrine _shewing_ incorruptness, gravity, sincerity," Titus 2:7

Prayer: Lord, help me to be a good example of your love to those who are unloving to me.

🍷 240

I was watching my grandson play with his toys. He was holding them upside-down in order to pretend they were diving into water. As I watched him, I was reminded of how we have to be upside-down when we dive into the real water. We will never be able to reach the water if we hang on to the diving board.

As I thought about this today, I was aware that there are many times when our lives feel like everything is upside-down. You know, those times when nothing seems to be going right and we are having trouble even thinking straight because we have so many different issues coming at us all at once.

Some people are very capable of walking to the end of the board and diving beautifully into the abyss below, but some of us, (I'm sure I'm not the only one), need to have support and encouragement, not only to get to the end of the board, but to be able to dive headlong into the depths of what God has for us.

So, sometimes when things feel as if they are upside-down, I wonder if it isn't God holding us there, helping us to dive into a new venture or area of our lives. When we land, it will not be a pretend life or venture. It will be very real, and God will be there with us all the way.

> **"Lo, I am with you alway, *even* unto the end of the world. Amen."**
> **Matthew 28:20b.**

Prayer: Lord, show me how to dive for your glory.

🍷 241

I was driving into town for a dental visit. On the way down the highway, I notice an ambulance parked on the side of the road. Ok, someone in that house is very ill and I prayed for them. Not any great long prayer, just what I call a Nehemiah prayer. Then I noticed two Police Officers standing talking to a couple. Alright, this is odd I thought. Then I finally pulled level at the next intersection and noticed glass on the road. "Oh, dear there has been an accident here, they really should do something about this corner, it is dangerous". Most locals know this and avoid it but sometimes you just can't. I had no idea that it was my daughter and granddaughter that was involved in that accident until later that day when she rang me.

As I thanked Him, for His protection of my family, I asked why? Not why were they involved in the accident? But why didn't I see everything? I saw, the police, ambulance, the other people but not my own family? She saw me drive past and it is as if they were hidden from my sight. God's response seems to be: "It doesn't matter how far away or how close you are, your children are in My hands now". Ecclesiastes 3:6 reminds me that there is:

"A time to get, and a time to lose; a time to keep, and a time to cast away;"

Prayer: Thank you for all the times you protect us and we don't even know it.

242

Due to some wet weather and a couple of busy weeks, I woke this morning to a long list of jobs that needed doing quickly and to a deadline. As I tried to do about three jobs at the same time, my stomach started complaining about the fact that I still hadn't eaten breakfast. So, I grab a piece of chocolate slice and a cuppa in order to get me through until I actually had time to sit down and eat my proper breakfast. It's what we call eating on the "run". It's something that most mothers with young children would be familiar with. Eating mouthfuls of food while making lunches, doing hair, making sure teeth are cleaned and bags are packed.

As I rushed around, I wondered if we are sometimes guilty of eating our spiritual food on the run. Are we so busy that we are only taking mouthfuls of God's word on the run? Don't get me wrong, small bits are better than nothing at all, but, being able to sit, enjoy and savour it makes it much easier to understand and hear what God is trying to tell us.

"All scripture *is* given by inspiration of God, and *is* profitable for doctrine, for reproof, for correction, for instruction in righteousness:" 2 Timothy 3:16

Prayer: Lord, let me take the time to learn from you properly and slowly.

243

There was quite a chill in the air this morning when I woke up. There wasn't a frost, but it was definitely cooler. It was a welcome change, after the hot steamy weather earlier in the week. Yet, as the day progressed, the temperature rose.

Thinking about the changing temperatures, I thought about how our lives rise and fall just like the daily temperature. There are times when I need to wrap myself up in the Word of God. They are the days when I can feel the chilling effects of sin and when my world seems to be out of control. There will always be days like that, not just chilly, but positively freezing. Yet, I need to remember that God is still there watching me

There are other times when life is good, and good things just seem to flow on through me and I experience that relaxed feeling of just being in Christ as I move forward each day working for Him. These warmer days in the spirit of God are to be enjoyed as they are a blessing from the Father, and I recognize that special feeling of fellowship with my Lord.

If I look to Jesus, there will always be something to learn from what I am undergoing.

"It is He who changes the times and the epochs; He removes kings and establishes kings; He gives wisdom to wise men and knowledge to men of understanding." Daniel 2:21.

Prayer: Lord, let me remember that you are in charge of my life and the world.

♛ 244

Wants, are very different to needs.

"But my God shall supply all your need according to his riches in glory by Christ Jesus." Philippians 4:19

I sometimes want to have more money, but then I would probably waste it. I want my house to be finished but then it could get destroyed by storm or fire. I could even want my books to be bestsellers, but then I might have to cope with much more attention than I want. I have often wanted a stress-free life, but then I wouldn't have learned nearly as much as I have. I could wish for a garden that has no weeds, but then how would I get some exercise. I might even want to live on the mountain tops for my entire life, but then I would miss the beauty of the valley shadows. I occasionally want to have spiritual gifts that would enable me to answer questions quickly and smartly. If I am honest though, my greatest want would be to be able to have a face to face conversation with my mother, to have her arms around me again. That is one want that is just not going to happen until I join her in Heaven. I still miss her love, wisdom, and care.

"And though I have *the gift of* prophecy, and understand all mysteries, and all knowledge; and though I have all faith so that I could remove mountains, and have not charity, I am nothing." 1 Corinthians 13:2.

Prayer: Lord, help me to know the difference between wants and needs.

245

Without water, living things just cannot survive for very long. Being that it is such a basic element of life meant that Jesus could use its relevance to living with great effect when He was trying to explain difficult subjects to his listeners, and to us.

When we moved to the farm, we had five children, three of them girls with long hair, and a grandson, all living together. We had four tanks as our water supply. When we had purchased the farm there was a shower in the bathroom. I told my husband that it had to go because I knew that the water supply would not be able to cope otherwise. We had to save water in whatever ways we could.

We were not there very long before the available supply had run out. The tanks were empty. New friends were very kind and helped us fix up a temporary pumping system from a well some distance from the house. It worked ok but had its issues. I remember one day, asking God to help us find a suitable solution to this problem.

My husband had already been inspired by with a very good solution, all we needed was sufficient funds to make it happen, which in due course, we managed to find. During this last drought, our dams have all but gone dry and even our wonderful waterhole solution struggled to keep pace with the water needs of our stock, but it did!

"*But* verily God hath heard *me*; he hath attended to the voice of my prayer." Psalm 66:19

Prayer: Lord, I thank you for all those answers that you have prepared for us even before we ask.

246

Weekends are, for many, non-existent. As farmers will attest to this, particularly during droughts. Weekends mean that the stock still needs to be fed, dams need to be checked, bogged stock pulled out of the mud, and cows milked if you live on a dairy farm.

For shift workers, weekends often mean working and the number of occupations being converted to this seems to be increasing. A few years back, no one would ever imagine sales staff working on shifts. For hospital staff, police, and ambulance workers the weekends are a time they dread as their workloads increase dramatically.

When my father was a boy, for most workers, weekends only consisted of Saturday afternoon and Sunday. Sunday was the day of rest for almost everyone. It was expected that you would attend a church service and spend time with the family, it was considered a day of worship.

When God created the world, even He rested for a day. **(Genesis 2:2-3)**. His perfection meant that we didn't need to toil, but once this was broken we had to work. This means that time needs to be set aside to rest and worship our God **(Exodus 34:21, Exodus 20:9 and Deuteronomy 5:13).**

We should worship our Lord every day, regardless of whether we are working or not, but we also need to rest from our work and I understand that for working people, that day could be any day during the week not just Sunday.

Prayer: Lord, let me worship you in all that I do, not just in church.

247

I wish for a mansion, not an earthly one, although I must admit that I like looking at those that have been built here.

When I tell you that I wish for my heavenly mansion, I'm not saying that I want it now. After all, I also hope that I have plenty of work to do for the

Lord first but I have just walked through a dark valley this last couple of weeks, and that mansion seemed a little closer at times.

This much I do know; when I get to see it, it will be finished, it will be beautiful, in fact, it will be stunning, and it will be mine.

John 14:2-3 says "In my Father's house are many mansions: if *it were* not *so*, I would have told you. I go to prepare a place for you. And if I go and prepare a place for you, I will come again, and receive you unto myself; that where I am, *there* ye may be also."

I have recently become aware of just how much we cannot know what our future is going to be, simply because we do not have foresight. We shake our heads at the disciples for their lack of insight, but here we are 2000 years later, and things are still happening differently to what they thought it would be. Walking by faith just means that we do not speculate but accept that: IT WILL BE.

Prayer: Lord, I thank you that you keep all your promises.

⸸ 248

Happiness is often found in memories. Particularly, this month we as a family remember so many members who have passed away during this time of year. Yes, today I particularly remember my mother, who passed away in 2014, but other members of the family are also remembering brothers, uncles, fathers, grandmothers, grandfathers, husbands, and children. They all have their memories to treasure and I pray that they will find good ones, hang on to them and smile through their sadness.

"Blessed *are* they that mourn: for they shall be comforted." Matthew 5:4.

We have been comforted by our good memories and the hope that we have in the resurrection of Jesus Christ.

Prayer: Lord, you gave us memories to help us remember the good things and to learn from the difficult things.

♛ 249

One man's trash is another man's treasure, isn't that the way the saying goes? Someone else can put what someone finds useless, to good use. A few years ago, I managed to lose a fair amount of weight, I had clothes that no longer fitted me and were uncomfortable because they were too big. It was time to buy some things that would fit me, and give those clothes to someone else who would be able to use them. I remember searching through a second-hand shop once and finding a glass bowl the same as one that we had been given as a wedding gift and had been broken.

I am often surprised to see the things that are important to some people. I am also surprised at what someone considers trash.

However, the greatest treasure is souls, for the Kingdom of God.

"But lay up for yourselves treasures in heaven, where neither moth nor rust doth corrupt, and where thieves do not break through nor steal:"
Matthew 6:20

Prayer: Lord, may I always remember what is a real treasure.

♛ 250

I know that our world needs more Love, Joy, and Peace. So many people try to find these things in different ways. Some people try to find love in relationships that end badly and are often only instigated through a blur of hurt. There are those that try to find joy in what they do, working hard, being the best, playing sport, or shopping until they drop. Finding peace, well, many try to crawl away and hide, while others use drug induced sleep to try and help. But it doesn't work!

On a state, federal and global level, governments also try to make these things a reality. They try to generate love by having conferences where leaders are supposed to talk and come to an agreement over many different issues. Joy is supposed to be created when they spend great sums of money on sporting events such as the Olympic, Commonwealth, and Asia Pacific games. To make peace, all they seem to do is make economic or military war. But again, it's not working!

We need to accept Love,

"Greater love hath no man than this, that a man lay down his life for his friends." John 15:13

We need to absorb Joy,

"These things have I spoken unto you, that my joy might remain in you, and *that* your joy might be full." John 15:11

We need to receive Peace,

"Peace I leave with you, my peace I give unto you: not as the world giveth, give I unto you. Let not your heart be troubled, neither let it be afraid." John 14:27

<u>**Prayer:**</u> Jesus, give us these three things, Love, Joy, and Peace.

🍷 251

I was getting many of those annoying phone calls. The phone would ring, I would answer it, the call would drop out, and I was left listening to the engaged signal. My response after about the first twelve calls was one of frustration.

I have to wonder how many times God calls us and doesn't get through. He calls people to come to Him and be saved. Every day the message is going out to all of humanity. He calls through His creation and His word.

Like those phone calls, He keeps calling, no matter how long we ignore Him. That is, of course, until we come to the end of our time here on earth, then there will be no more time to answer that call.

"If we confess our sins, he is faithful and just to forgive us *our* sins, and to cleanse us from all unrighteousness." 1 John 1:9

If we answer that call and learn from Him, He will help us to develop the fruits of the spirit, as listed in Galatians 5:22,
"But the fruit of the Spirit is love, joy, peace, longsuffering, gentleness, goodness, faith,"

Prayer: Thank you for never giving up on us.

252

I'm sitting in my lovely sunny spot, thinking, writing, and being very grateful. And... I'm thinking about how it almost always takes a close call for people to start taking action. I have known, and hated, a particular corner for many years but I have avoided using that intersection rather than making my concerns known. But I nearly lost my granddaughter, and I could have lost my daughter, and suddenly I wanted something done. I ask myself if someone else's family had been involved, would I be so determined to be heard?

I look at the table beside me and see the mess it's in and realize that I in particular, and maybe all of us, are too prone, even on a world scale, to cleaning up messes rather than not creating the mess in the first place. There are a few industries where creating is still going on, but on most levels, it seems that we think it's been done or it's someone else's problem.

"How then shall they call on him in whom they have not believed? and how shall they believe in him of whom they have not heard? and how shall they hear without a preacher?" Romans 10:14.

Prayer: Let me think before I make a mess, so no one has to clean up after me.

🍷 253

The colour yellow stands for freshness, happiness, positivity, clarity, energy, optimism, enlightenment, remembrance, intellect, honour, loyalty, and joy. I guess it's no accident that the sun, that wakes us up in the morning, is also yellow in colour, or that the flames of a fire that help keep us warm and happy in winter are yellow as well.

Have you noticed that many types of flowers also have a yellow variety, in its various hues and if you see them in a garden, they add a bright splash of colour?

People we meet who have a positive outlook, often referred to as a 'sunny disposition' on life, will also uplift us and help us meet any challenges we have to face.

"A cheerful heart makes good medicine,
but a crushed spirit dries up the bones." Proverbs 17:22.

Prayer: Lord, help me to bring sunshine into someone's life today.

🍷 254

Quietness, meditation, relaxation, and calmness seem to be the requirements of Zen. Well, I am a farmer's wife with five children, eight grandchildren, and one great-grandchild. Apart from my husband, they do not live permanently under my roof, but there is still a lot of busyness in my life. Sometimes, finding time to meditate, relax, and pray can be very difficult. I know I have mentioned this before, and I am not sorry that I need to repeat it, but apart from the last thing at night, the best times I have to do these things are when I am washing up or gardening. These are the times when I can be fairly sure that I will be left alone. I use to take these opportunities to talk to my Lord and Saviour about my earthly friends who I know are struggling. I also ask Him to bless those who have taken the trouble to purchase my book.

"Blessed *is* the man that walketh not in the counsel of the ungodly, nor standeth in the way of sinners, nor sitteth in the seat of the scornful. But his delight *is* in the law of the LORD, and in his law doth, he meditates day and night. And he shall be like a tree planted by the rivers of water, that bringeth forth his fruit in his season; his leaf also shall not wither, and whatsoever he doeth shall prosper." Psalm 1:1-3

Challenge: To mediate on the word of God until we can face life, relaxed in Him.

255

There is a place that I stop at when I am traveling north, however, I always approach the door with fear and trepidation. I know that the business has been on the market for quite a few years now, so, I am always afraid that it has been sold. These people have been such a blessing to me. They reached out to me at a time when I was completely shattered. I had stopped there for a break. When my food was delivered, they could have just placed the food in front of me with a smile and moved on to the next customer, but they didn't.

When I remember the way that they engaged with me in my time of despair, and every other time since, I am reminded of how James talks about how an active faith is proved in the way people work.

"What use is it, my brethren, if someone says he has faith but he has no works? Can that faith save him? If a brother or sister is without clothing and in need of daily food, and one of you says to them, "Go in peace, be warmed and be filled," and yet you do not give them what is necessary for *their* body, what use is that? Even so, faith, if it has no works, is dead, *being* by itself." James 2:14-17 (NAS).

Do I want them to sell? No, because I will miss their kindness on future visits. However, I must not be selfish, so now I'm asking God to bless them with more blessings than I can imagine.

Prayer: Your plans for everyone are as unique as they are, thank you for all the different people that you bring into my life, even if it is for a short time.

♈ 256

There is a lot of talk around the world at present in view of what has happened in the Middle East, yet there doesn't seem to be a lot of action. What can we do to help and fix this problem, not a lot physically but we can pray, pray and pray some more?

The real solution to these problems is in the revival of people from the inside out, not external forces. Yes, we will have to pray about what it is that God wants us to do and there are voices out there that will tell us that we are not making a difference but God sees everything that we do no matter how small it is.

"For this very reason, make every effort to supplement your faith with virtue, and virtue with knowledge, and knowledge with self-control, and self-control with steadfastness, and steadfastness with godliness, and godliness with brotherly affection, and brotherly affection with love. For if these qualities are yours and are increasing, they keep you from being ineffective or unfruitful in the knowledge of our Lord Jesus Christ." 2 Peter 1:5-8 (ESV).

Prayer: Lord, show me what you want me to do for you

257

I had developed another health issue and I wasn't happy. I had just finished recovering from the last one and I wanted to stay well and healthy, something that, I suppose, is not really possible at my age. However, on this particular morning I was so busy moaning about the issue that I nearly forgot to take the medicine that is supposed to help fix the problem.

God tapped me on the shoulder again. There is no point moaning about an issue if you don't do something about it. There are, of course, times when you are unable to do a thing but, when the solution is right there, it's time to get up and get moving. Not only did I take my medicine, but I managed to get outside and started work on my garden, which needed a lot of problems fixed.

The greatest difficulty is knowing when to find a solution and when to walk away.

> "**Happy *is* the man *that* findeth wisdom, and the man *that* getteth understanding.**" **Proverbs 3:13.**

Prayer: Lord, may I find the wisdom that comes from your word.

258

Isn't Heaven going to be a wonderful place? I know this because, recently, I had a washing machine replaced as a result of an unexpected response from the store that I had purchased the previous machine from. We had the old machine for six years but it just didn't do the job properly. It would become unbalanced during the spin cycle and would leave more dirt in the clothes than it took out. Some clothes actually came out dirtier than they went in.

What I realized after the new machine had completed two loads of washing, was that I had got to the point of actually dreading doing the washing. It was doing such a good job that I now look forward to washing, and in fact, I found myself searching for things to put into the new machine.

If a new machine makes such a difference here on earth, how much more beautiful is Heaven going to be, as it will be a place where everything works, and works perfectly.

"And God shall wipe away all tears from their eyes; and there shall be no more death, neither sorrow, nor crying, neither shall there be any more pain: for the former things are passed away". Revelation 21:4

Prayer. Thank you for giving us a small taste of what Heaven might look like, so we can look forward to going there.

259

I was weeding my garden, again! It's a large part of my exercise program. I was still working on a particular section which seemed to have a lot of weeds. What I discovered was that when I pulled the weeds out by the roots, a large part of the problem was removed as well.

I thought about our lives and how, when we get to the root of the problems we have and remove them there, we solve a good many other issues. So, when Jesus forgives us and removes sin from our lives, it makes a positive impact on so many different levels. If Jesus removes our anger, it will have a bearing on how we relate to family members, people in the street, drivers on the road, and workmates. It leaves room for other things to come into our lives and make us a greater influence for Him.

"Now the deeds of the flesh are evident, which are: immorality, impurity, sensuality, idolatry, sorcery, enmities, strife, jealousy, outbursts of anger,

disputes, dissensions, factions, envying, drunkenness, carousing, and things like these, of which I forewarn you, just as I have forewarned you, that those who practice such things will not inherit the kingdom of God. But the fruit of the Spirit is love, joy, peace, patience, kindness, goodness, faithfulness, gentleness, self-control; against such things, there is no law. Now those who belong to Christ Jesus have crucified the flesh with its passions and desires." Galatians 5:19-24 (NAS).

Prayer: Lord, I thank you for being the perfect gardener of my life and for knowing exactly what the best thing for me is.

260

I have a pretty jug that I decided to use recently. I heard it crack and, after careful examination, I eventually found the cracks. My instinct was to throw it out. After all, that is what it was made for, if it cannot be used as a jug, it is useless, right? Well, maybe not. As I looked, I saw that it was still pretty, so I recycled my jug.

As I was thinking about what to do with the jug, it also occurred to me that we, as human beings, are also cracked. We have all sinned; we are no longer the people that God created back in the Garden of Eden. Yes, some of our cracks may be hard to see by those around us, but God can see them all. Yet, just as I love the jug, so God loves us more. Regardless of how broken we are or feel, He can still use us to bring glory to His name and we can still worship Him by doing what we can, working with what we have, and carrying out those duties to the best of our abilities.

My jug now brings a new perfume into our house, it's full of Lavender, and it doesn't need to hold water, it just holds the lavender stalks. When we allow God to use us in whatever way He wants, we will bring a new fragrance into our world. No, we may not be doing what we were created for, but we are still loved and cared for by our Lord and Saviour.

"The lord is nigh unto them that are of a broken heart, and saveth such as be of a contrite spirit" Psalm 34:18.

<u>*Prayer:*</u> Lord, show me where I can bring perfume to someone who needs some encouragement.

♆ 261

My husband bought me a second-hand washing machine before I got sick. This meant that making sure that it worked didn't happen for a few months. If we had been able to take our time, we would have worked out that all it needed was a new lid. I look back on this experience with some regret because, if I had listened to God properly, I would have had a new TV as well as a working washing machine, which would have made my life a little easier.

When we are accepting the gifts we are given throughout the year, not only at Christmas time, do we accept them as an undeserved favour or do we have an attitude of entitlement. Some people give me the impression that they are entitled to receive only good things in this world. In the lead up to Christmas, I hear so many talks on TV about what to do with those unwanted gifts you receive. Give them to charity, or re-gift them to others.

God made available to us, a gift that cost Him so much, was so underserved by us, and one that we don't even have to accept if we don't want to, but He doesn't re-gift it to others, and He certainly doesn't throw it in the charity bin. He leaves it there, available for us to accept at any time. Of course, if we don't accept that gift, there will be eternal consequences.

"Freely you received, freely give." Matthew 10:8b (NAS).

<u>*Prayer:*</u> Thank you for your free gift of salvation, even though it cost you so much.

262

Around our home, we have a particular variety of bird that tends to create a lot of mess. They are a wonderful host for those horrid things called lice. Some people consider them to be only a pest.

Yet, they are special to God, so special that they are specifically mentioned in the Bible at least five times. Yes, they are sparrows.

"Are not five sparrows sold for two cents? Yet not one of them is forgotten before God." Luke 12:6 (NAS).

It has been suggested that we need to try and get rid of them, but I know that we cannot get rid of them without putting all the other small birds at risk.

1 Timothy 2:3-4 "For this *is* good and acceptable in the sight of God our Saviour; Who will have all men to be saved, and to come unto the knowledge of the truth."

This verse tells us that Jesus came to earth to make salvation available to everyone. Not just the good people, not just the rich people, not just the people of one nationality. He came to save all mankind and yes, that includes women and children as well.

Do you feel like a sparrow, useless and a pest? *Well, guess what!* Jesus came to save you and you are so special to Him. Come to Him today, He will accept you, mess and all; He loves you just the way you are.

"For God so loved the world, that he gave his only begotten Son, that whosoever believeth in him should not perish, but have everlasting life."
John 3:16

Challenge: Remember what some people see as pests, God sees as being very special.

🍷 263

A young person was telling me that they had visited a Psychic. They started the conversation with, "I know you don't believe in them, but they told me......".

The thing is, I do believe that these people exist and can see things that are withheld from others. However, I do feel sad for those who depend on these sightings to live their lives. The problem is that they don't always get it right. Even if they were right, it's not a way I would want to live. For instance, I don't want to know how long I am going to live for. It would be too easy for me to put off doing some very important jobs. God wants us to live as if each day was our last and not put off all those important decisions that involve our relationship with Him and spreading the gospel to those around us.

God is the only person who can truly see the future, He has yours and mine in His hands and we can trust Him to give us the best there is in life, without knowing what it is.

Walking by faith means that we take each day as it comes, we trust Jesus to lead us, comfort us, and give us the strength to get through that day.

"For we walk by faith, not by sight:" 2 Corinthians 5:7.

Prayer: Lord, help me to trust in you and you alone.

🍷 264

Not long ago, mail meant that you got a message, written on paper, enclosed in an envelope, and delivered by a Postman. This postman walked from house to house, twice a day and put the letter in your mailbox. If you sent a letter, you would place it in the post office's box and your letter would get to the required destination. You would then wait for a few days to get a reply.

In Australia, the mail travelled great distances on horseback, train, and stream boat long before there was any aircraft. People have told me that the service then, was more reliable than it is today.

When I send a request out to my Lord, all I have to do is ask, simply and quietly, and He hears me. He may take a long time to give me an answer, but that answer will be perfect for me when it comes.

"But when ye pray, use not vain repetitions, as the heathen *do*: **for they think that they shall be heard for their much speaking. Be not ye, therefore, like unto them: for your Father knoweth what things ye have need of, before ye ask him" Matthew 6:7-8.**

Prayer: Lord, I thank you for always hearing me.

265

There are so many different sorts of mail now. "Junk-mail" is from companies advertising their goods and services. They send them to your mailbox, telling you what they want you to buy. There are those nasty "bills" that scare me when we don't have the money to pay them. At special times like Christmas, birthdays, or a wedding, the occasional card might arrive.

Of course, there is that new one, called Email. With the increased use of email, we have decided to dub the original form of mail as "snail mail". Most correspondence today is carried out through cyberspace. It's faster, more efficient, and allows an instant response as long as the internet service is working properly.

As a result, the traditional mail now takes even longer, because their services have been downsized due to smaller demand, maybe this is why it's been dubbed "Snail Mail".

Prayer is our mail service to God. It isn't slow. It isn't advertising or asking God for what we want. It isn't a bill either, recompense for our service to Him. Prayer is a conversation with a friend, one who gave the greatest gift of love, salvation! This mail service will never be downsized.

"Pray without ceasing." 1 Thessalonians 5:17.

Prayer: Thank you for always answering my prayers, even if it's not the way I would like.

266

There is a saying that goes a bit like "the harder I work, the luckier I get". There is no doubt that just existing on this earth is hard work most days. Some people work very hard all their lives and it would appear to most of us that they never get a "lucky break". It's nice to know that, while God does not promise us an easy, comfortable, and wealthy existence here on earth, He does promise to walk with us, help us, and give us the strength to meet the challenges that are sent our way. I'm not lucky, I am a child of God and His faithfulness is guaranteed!

"Know therefore that the LORD thy God, he _is_ God, the faithful God, which keepeth covenant and mercy with them that love him and keep his commandments to a thousand generations;" Deuteronomy 7:9

Prayer: Oh Lord, I give you praise for choosing me to be your child.

267

Have you heard it said: "But for the grace of God go I"? There are no guarantees in this life. It even appears that some of the guarantees that you get with goods and services are not worth the paper they're written on. There are so many people and businesses these days who think nothing of breaking their word and sadly, some of these people can be found in the congregations of our churches.

As I write this, I am coming to terms with one of those phone calls where I was told that my computer has been hacked into and was doing nasty things. The caller wanted me to fix it while they talked me through the process. It didn't matter how many times I hung up on them, they kept ringing me back. Leaving me feeling quite exhausted from the incident. There was no guarantee that they were who they said they were. In the end, I had to ask them to call me back tomorrow. I am hoping that they got the message. It was a dishonest scam of course, which I reported.

I am so glad that God, is honest, faithful to His promises, and will never scam anyone.

"Faithful is he that calleth you, who also will do it." 1 Thessalonians 5:24.

Prayer: May I never forget that your gifts are your acts of grace towards me.

268

I like staying up late at night. I often think, pray, and write better when the house is quiet and I don't have other distractions crowding in on my time. I am definitely a night owl. If I'm not working, I'm watching TV or reading.

I remember being told as a child, "Early to bed and early to rise, makes a man healthy, wealthy and wise." Some research revealed that "The length and precision of this 18th-century proverb leaves little room for interpretation as to its meaning". Like many improving mottos, for example 'a rolling stone gathers no moss' and 'a stitch in time saves nine', it was an encouragement to hard, diligent work. The earliest record of it that I can find in print is in _Poor Richard's Almanack_, which was an annual journal published by Benjamin Franklin under the pseudonym of Poor Richard between 1732 and 1758.

The message was that if you worked hard and slept well, you would be rewarded. I will always be a night owl, working, praying, and writing well into the early hours of the morning, but that is ok because that's the way God made me.

"And whatsoever ye do, do *it* heartily, as to the Lord, and not unto men;" Colossians 3:23.

Prayer: Lord, whatever I do, the most important thing is that I bring glory to you.

🍷 269

One of the mysteries of life is that, often, opposites attract, and this has been the case with my husband and I. He is a morning person through and through. Five-thirty seems to set off some alarm in his head and he has to be out of bed doing something. These days I'm pleased that the alarm has reset itself to 6.30 am. What do we call these people, Morning Larks?

To him, the early morning is the best part of the day. It is fresh, clean, quiet, and usually cool. I get his point of view; I just appreciate sleep better in the mornings.

I see it as a balance thing, he looks after things in the mornings and I look after things at night, that way we cover the whole day together.

Thankfully our Lord never sleeps, He is awake all night watching over the whole of His creation.

"Behold, he that keepeth Israel shall neither slumber nor sleep." Psalm 121:4

Prayer: Lord, I thank you for watching over me all the time.

🍷 270

I love a lot of things; my family, writing and reading, and sometimes I even *like* them as well. During a time when life was very stressful, I found that it would have been very easy for me to hate things and people that I am supposed to love. What I had to do was come to terms with the fact that no matter how I felt, I had to do something. Love them; I didn't have to trust them. After all, Jesus loves us, no matter how we feel about Him.

"But love ye your enemies, and do good, and lend, hoping for nothing again; and your reward shall be great, and ye shall be the children of the Highest: for he is kind unto the unthankful and *to* the evil." Luke 6:35.
Prayer: Lord, may I love as you have loved me, unconditionally.

271

As a child, I was taught that Sunday was a day of rest for everyone, therefore, I find myself debating the rights and wrongs of shopping on Sundays. It is obvious that if we buy goods on Sunday, we are forcing others to work on Sunday. However, when we buy goods on Monday, we are still forcing people to work on Sunday. For instance, to be able to purchase a newspaper on Monday, staff members have worked on Sunday.

As we live out of town, I often found it hard to keep enough food in the cupboards over the weekend while the children were attending school. It, therefore, became necessary for me to purchase food after church on Sunday, in order to have enough food for lunches on Monday.

A Christian friend encouraged me by saying, "God allows acts of mercy to be carried out on Sunday and buying food for your children would be considered an act of mercy".

One would hope that by shopping on Sunday, I am carrying out an act of mercy for the staff who need the extra hours to provide them with enough money to live.

While some may call this a bit of a stretch, Jesus carried out many acts of mercy for many people, including healing a man with a crippled hand. **Matthew 12:9-13**.

"Therefore, it is lawful to do good on the Sabbath day." Matthew 12:12b

Prayer: Lord, I pray that I will be a blessing by being cheerful when I shop, even on a Sunday.

🍷 272

There are times when I want to have a fairy godmother, like Cinderella, unfortunately, real stories have very different endings.

Some end in tragedy; some have good endings, while others will have unexpected outcomes. The truth is that we all write our own story. A few years ago, when you played certain DVDs, you were able to decide which ending you wanted.

We all have characters and events woven into our story. How we respond to those characters and events will affect the ending of our story. We can push our way through all the challenges that life will dish up or we can give up, sit down, and cry. What we cannot expect, is to have a fairy godmother to come along and fix every problem that we face. Even when we make mistakes, we can pick ourselves up, dust ourselves off, and continue to move forward. We cannot expect the consequences to disappear and not affect the future chapters of our story.

"And every man that striveth for the mastery is temperate in all things. Now they *do it* to obtain a corruptible crown, but we an incorruptible. I therefore so run, not as uncertainly; so, fight I, not as one that beateth the air." 1 Corinthians 9:25-26.

Prayer: May my story tell of your goodness to me.

🍷 273

They say that eyes are the windows to the soul. Eyes will tell you if a person is joking around, serious, sick, sad, angry, or in a world of their own.

When I was little, we had a couple of sayings for those who were in a world of their own. When we really look at people and see the message in their eyes, we are only seeing a snapshot of them. We can only see what they are feeling at that precise moment. When we walk away from their company, we cannot see the pain, drama, or joy that they experience while we are not in their presence.

Psalm 139:1-8 says: "O LORD, thou hast searched me, and known *me*. Thou knowest my down sitting and mine uprising, thou understandest my thought afar off. Thou compassest my path and my lying down, and art acquainted *with* all my ways. For *there is* not a word in my tongue, *but*, lo, O LORD, thou knowest it altogether. Thou hast beset me behind and before, and laid thine hand upon me. *Such* knowledge *is* too wonderful for me; it is high, I cannot *attain* unto it. Whither shall I go from thy spirit? or whither shall I flee from thy presence? If I ascend up into heaven, thou *art* there: if I make my bed in hell, behold, thou *art* there."

Prayer: What a wonderful thing, Lord, that you see all this and more!

274

Have you ever thought about the life of those people you look up to, those famous TV stars, authors, or celebrities? Their followers read and see what they want people to see but rarely, if ever, do you get to see into their hearts, into what really makes them who they are. Yes, you might see something of their heart in the words an author writes, but it is only a snapshot, it is only what is there at the time of writing.

What we never see is the dirty dishes in the sink, the laundry full of washing, the kids' bedroom mess. You don't get to see their hurt, pains, and heartaches. They are regular people, they have to wash dishes, shower, and wash their clothes just like the rest of us. God made them, in the same way He made you and me.

They may seem special to us, but we are just as special to God because He treats all of His creation equally.

"There is neither Jew nor Greek, there is neither bond nor free, there is neither male nor female: for ye are all one in Christ Jesus." Galatians 3:28.

Prayer: Lord, I thank you that I am special in your sight, just as special as everyone else.

♀ 275

These days, we go shopping and pick our groceries off the shelf, put them in a trolley, and pay for them at a checkout. It is so easy, convenient, and reliable. What we don't see, and often forget about, is the Farmer who worked hard behind the scenes the make sure that the supply is dependable. We don't get to see farmers, their wives, and often, their children, working the long hours alongside each other. We do not see the drama of animals having to be cared for and saved from predators. They work in all sorts of weather; they pray daily for the protection of their crops and animals. They put in long hours in the office and the paddock. Yet, if the food was to disappear from the supermarket shelves, we would notice. Then we would ask "where does this come from, what has gone wrong?" It is easy to take our food, and farmers for granted because they are always there.

We often do the same thing to God. He is always there, He makes the sun rise, the stars shine, rain to fall, and plants grow. He is always there working behind the scenes. It is easy to take Him for granted. It will never happen but what if we woke up one morning to find the sun had disappeared?

"The heavens declare the glory of God; and the firmament sheweth his handiwork." Psalm 19:1

Prayer: Lord, help me not to take anyone or anything for granted.

276

I was reading a story recently; it was one of those stories where they tell two connected stories dovetailed together. Suddenly I stopped and reread the line I had just finished. Hum, I thought they have put the wrong character in here.

What aggravated me the most was how irritated I felt that they hadn't got the details right. It was a minor slip up, and it didn't take away from the story. I find it very easy to do this in other areas of my life as well. We get so caught up in details and issues, that we miss the context of life.

Now, don't get me wrong, I'm not saying that people shouldn't do a job properly, they should. Compassion is a good thing when mistakes are made, and we need to remember that no one is perfect.

Psalm 86:15 says: "But thou, O Lord, *art* a God full of compassion, and gracious, longsuffering, and plenteous in mercy and truth." And we are instructed in Ephesians 5:1-2 to **"Be ye, therefore, followers of God, as dear children; and walk in love, as Christ also hath loved us, and hath given himself for us an offering and a sacrifice to God for a sweet-smelling savour."**

<u>Prayer:</u> Lord, may I always look to the final outcome, not the unnecessary things of this world.

277

Sunday has traditionally been our day of rest in western society. These days, more and more people spend their Sundays at sport, beach, markets, chilling in front of the Television, or madly trying to get ready for the week ahead. I keep remembering a story in my first book about a man whose doctor recommend that he attend church in order to get some rest. I understand that it may have worked at the time, but certainly not now.

The bible tells me in Exodus 34:21

"Six days thou shalt work, but on the seventh day thou shalt rest: in earing time and in harvest thou shalt rest."

As a mother, I found this very hard. Do we have a legalistic view of "rest"? Once I did the maths and worked out that if I spent a certain amount of time resting each day, I could cover the full day. It was an effort to spread the rest out over my very busy week at a time when Sunday seemed to be the most demanding.

I had a feeling during the week that God was trying to get me to lift my game up a notch or two.

"And whatsoever ye do in word or deed, [do] all in the name of the Lord Jesus, giving thanks to God and the Father by him". Colossians 3:17

<u>Prayer:</u> Lord, whether I am busy or resting, may I still give you the glory.

278

If there is one temptation that I find hard to resist, it is "quitting". When things get tough, I just want to sit down and quit. I find it easier to look at that very distant finish line, and think about how hard life is going to be, before I can even get somewhere near it. I have to take a deep breath before I can say "no, don't quit, just take this one step at a time." One small step will get me just a little closer to the finish line.

Life can be tough for each of us. Some people seem to have a tough life from beginning to end. Others appear to have a series of difficult years in a row.

There are times when it is necessary to sit and rest awhile, I know that, otherwise God would not have instructed us to:

"Be still, and know that I *am* God:" Psalm 46:10a

Resting is very different to quitting. By not quitting, I have learned a lot of things; I do have courage, strength, organizational skills, patience, a reasonable imagination, and best of all, understanding. This allows me to sympathise with others.

"Have not I commanded thee? Be strong and of a good courage; be not afraid, neither be thou dismayed: for the LORD thy God *is* with thee whithersoever thou goest." Joshua 1:9.

Prayer: Lord, help me to listen to you when I feel like quitting.

279

Diets, what a variety there are available to us. You can have low carb, gluten free, low fat, high protein, just to name a few. We hear so many instructions about how much to eat, what not to eat, and how not to overindulge.

When we read the Bible, we are eating our spiritual food. Thankfully, we can eat all day, every day, and seven days a week and still more if we could. This is one time when it doesn't matter how much we eat; we will never overindulge or do any harm.

"Thy words were found, and I did eat them; and thy word was unto me the joy and rejoicing of mine heart: for I am called by thy name, O LORD God of hosts." Jeremiah 15:16.

Prayer: Lord, let me read your word as if I am starving and become stronger as I devour it.

280

I had a dream one night about having two lives. In one life, I lived in another town, was mean, and had a rap sheet. In the other, the one I was living, I was nice, kind, and happy. I have a father who loves me. Somehow, I find out about this other life and my father in my new life is more than willing to help me when I ring the station to turn myself into the Police.

As I thought about the dream during the next day, I wondered what it might mean. The more I thought about it, the more I realized that it could be like our lives, one will be here on earth, the other in Heaven.

Yes, I have a rap sheet, I think bad thoughts, I'm cranky, mean, and have ignored God but He is willing to help me, just like the father in my dream. My new life is like the eternity that I will spend in Heaven and my bad life here on earth will be forgotten.

"Therefore, if any man *be* in Christ, *he is* a new creature: old things are passed away; behold, all things are become new." 2 Corinthians 5:17

Prayer: Lord, I thank you that you have erased my rap sheet through the blood of Jesus.

281

It was the height of summer and I suddenly realized that my roses were not flowering as they had the previous year. It wasn't because they hadn't had water, we had rain. What they hadn't been given, was care. I had been sick in the previous months and was unable to put in the time and energy to help them along. In order to make the roses flower in the way they had before, they needed my care, time, and energy.

So it is with people. Their Heavenly Father looks after them, but they also need care, time, and energy by those around them to make them grow and blossom into the beautiful person that God intended them to be.

"So, when they had dined, Jesus saith to Simon Peter, Simon, *son* of Jonas, lovest thou me more than these? He saith unto him, Yea, Lord; thou knowest that I love thee. He saith unto him, Feed my lambs". John 21:15.

That instruction is to us as well.

Prayer: Lord, help me to encourage those around me to grow in you.

282

I was thinking about prayer, how we often ask for something and just wait for the answer. Sometimes, we tell ourselves that we are exercising faith, but I wonder if sometimes it is actually laziness. I know I do this sometimes. Of course, there are times when we really do need to just sit and wait for God's time to come around but there are times when God wants us to participate in the process of answering that prayer.

In much the same way as a child comes to their parents and asks for a new toy, there are times when the parent says that the child needs to help by doing chores or saving pocket money in order to receive the desired toy. By participating in the process, the child will often appreciate their desire more.

I believe that it is the same with us, if we have worked or participated in the process of the answered prayer, we will treasure the outcome more highly.

If the widow that Jesus talks about in Luke 18:1-8 had sat down and waited, nothing would have happened.

"Yet because this widow troubleth me, I will avenge her, lest by her continual coming she weary me." verse 5.

We have to search, try, test and be open-minded about how God will answer our prayers and it is this process that will make us appreciate the prize more.

Prayer: Lord, help me to know when to wait and when to work.

283

What a beautiful picture we see in Isaiah 11:1-10. A picture of peace, love, and safety. The vision includes animals that are normally prey sitting down, unafraid, with their archrivals. It has traditionally been suggested that it's a picture of our future somewhere way into the distance. Even now, we cannot imagine a wolf not eating a lamb if it was sitting right next to it, or a lion eating straw like the ox, this would need a complete change of its genetic makeup. What of a child playing near a snake's nest, most adults would not be happy to see such a thing and most mothers would be horrified to see their children anywhere near snakes of any sort, let alone the deadly variety mentioned here.

What I do see in this passage is a wonderful picture of faith in action. God wants us to trust Him in the same way that this passage gives us the vision of the future. Calmly waiting for God to work and deal with all those troubles that come our way throughout our lives.

Prayer: Lord, let me trust you with an active faith, knowing that you will protect me, no matter what happens.

284

Our children arrive into this world and look at their parents with complete love and faith. They trust us with their lives, future, and well-being. The what-if's that we develop happen, as we, as children, are let down by adults, and things in our lives that don't go according to plan. A toy that breaks after it's been bashed around too much, the doll that falls apart after the tug-of-war has happened with the brother. The father that breaks his promise or mother who is just too busy to do what we want, when we want it to happen. This is when we start thinking about the what-ifs in life. By the time we become adults, we are often so caught up in the what-if's that we can lose faith in anyone and anything.

Yet, God our heavenly father/parent is never too busy and will always have our best interests in mind when He leads us. We may not always see that straight away. I was looking back over the last few years with one of my children recently and as we discussed where God had brought them, I could really see that God knew what was best for them.

"Your faithfulness endures to all generations; you have established the earth, and it stands fast." Psalms 119:9 (ESV).

Prayer: Lord, I thank you for knowing exactly what is best for me and all my family members.

285

There is nothing greater for God than for us to love and trust Him. To me this is one reason why Jesus was so disappointed in the disciples when they turned the children away. He wanted them to understand the value of their outlook on life and, just maybe, it was a good reminder that we can always learn from the children in the world. After all, they are the ones who are the first to see the good things in other children without looking at their appearance. They are often the first ones to stick up for someone being unfairly treated and they are often moved by the injustices they see around them. If we look at the children around us, we will see many of the things that God wants us to learn and understand.

"Trust in the LORD with all thine heart, and lean not unto thine own understanding." Proverbs 3:5

Prayer: Help me to trust you even when I do not understand where you are leading me.

🍷 286

On a recent trip, we were able to get away early and had plenty of time to get to our destination. I was surprised to discover that it really didn't feel like a long way, like it had on previous occasions when we were running late, or pushed for time. As I considered this, it occurred to me that the difference was in the perspective. God often requires us to change our perspective. He wants us to see things differently when he comes into our lives. Trials are not sent our way to break us but to make us stronger. Death is not the end but a doorway to eternity. These perspectives help us to increase our faith and teach us to trust God more.

"And we know that all things work together for good to them that love God, to them who are the called according to _his_ purpose." Romans 8:28.

Prayer: Lord, help me to see that you are helping me grow through all the things that happen in my life.

🍷 287

Since the death of my mother, I have become aware of just how much I don't know about Heaven. Some people will try and tell you that the Bible tells us all the things that are going to happen, in minute detail.

However, the Old Testament also told God's people about the arrival of Jesus in the same detail and yet, they were unable to see Jesus for who He was.

I'm pretty sure that human nature has not changed much in two thousand years and I have become very aware that the future is a great mystery to me.

I am aware that this means that God wants me to step into the future in faith, knowing that what He has planned is the best for me.

"Now faith is the substance of things hoped for, the evidence of things not seen." Hebrews 11:1.

Prayer: Lord, let me trust you for the present and the future.

288

I was thinking about a time when I was very disorganized and trying to finish lots of things at once. The result was that I didn't finish many projects and was constantly living in a chaotic mess. What God showed me was that I needed to reduce the things that I was trying to do. In other words, I needed to put off trying to do my craft work while I was working outside the home and wait until I had the time and money to do these things. I had to learn to be patient.

On a spiritual level, we can sometimes be tricked into doing the right thing at the wrong time. We try to witness to people long before the Holy Spirit has prepared them to receive the message we are giving them and all that is achieved is a lot more angst towards God, making the process longer.

It is so hard, when the ones we love are far from Him, to not do things that we think will bring them closer to God. However, sometimes we just have to step back and let Him use other resources to work the miracle in their lives.

"But seek ye first the kingdom of God, and his righteousness; and all these things shall be added unto you." Matthew 6:33.

Prayer: Lord, show me when to let go and let you work in the lives of the ones I love.

🍷 289

I was thinking about the weather. It related to the heat wave conditions we were experiencing and how we were told that there were more and more days of extreme temperatures. However, I am pretty sure that what we were being told are heat wave conditions, were only very hot days, when my grandparents were alive.

Even when I went to buy new clothes recently, I found that the size 8 that I would normally buy no longer fitted me. This isn't because I had gotten bigger, I was still wearing the size 8 clothes that I already owned. It appears that the manufacturers had shifted the bar.

As humans, we shift the bar up and down to suit ourselves, either to make ourselves, or others, feel happier but it really only ends up confusing us. Thankfully there is one person who never shifts the bar. Sin is sin, no matter how small or big it is and there is only ever going to be one way to get into Heaven.

"I am the way, the truth, and the life, no man cometh unto the Father, but by me" John 14:6.

Prayer: Lord, I thank you that your standards never change.

🍷 290

A family member was upset by something and proceeded to let anyone who would listen know just how upset they were. It wasn't long before I realized that I was also getting upset about the situation, not because the situation was unfair or wrong, but simply because the member of the family was upset. I ended up asking them not to discuss the matter anymore as the attitude was catching. On another occasion, I was feeling morbid and retreated to my bedroom to be by myself in case I affected the other members of the household with my gloominess.

> **"Finally, brethren, whatsoever things are true, whatsoever things are honest, whatsoever things are just, whatsoever things are pure, whatsoever things are lovely, whatsoever things are of good report; if there be any virtue, and if there be any praise, think on these things." Philippians 4:8.**

Prayer: Lord, help me to focus on the good things in my life and let me drown out the not so good things.

291

There are so many types of songs. Some are joyful, others are sad. They can be songs of victory or songs of lament. There are protest songs or, as I learned recently, there are even coded songs. These were songs sung by the slaves in America and contained coded messages in them for escaping slaves hiding nearby. They contained warnings of where to go in the swamps or if there were trackers nearby. Many of David's songs started off as sad, prayerful songs that eventually ended with victory notes.

What sort of song has God put into your heart today? Maybe, like David, it is one of lament, maybe you are singing sadly about guilt, conviction, or mourning a loved one. Maybe there is no victory in your song yet.

> **"He put a new song in my mouth, a song of praise to our God. Many will see and fear, and put their trust in him." Psalm 40:3 (ESV).**

Prayer: Lord, please give me a song even when I don't feel like singing.

292

Some mornings I turn the news on to find out what has happened while I have been sleeping. There are many mornings however, when I just want to turn it off very quickly because it appears to be all bad news, tragic in fact. Someone once commented that, in order to stay safe from illness and harm, we needed to become hermits. This would mean that we would stay home and never venture into town or mix with others.

My response was that we are not meant to do this, we are meant to step out in faith and trust God to look after us and give us the courage to carry on despite illness and/or disability. After all, it was only a few generations back when it didn't matter where you lived or what you did, you were confronted with illness and hardships every day and these people didn't stay hidden away from the problems they saw around them. They stepped out and worked hard, knowing full well that they might get ill and death was a possible consequence of their work.

"Take therefore no thought for the morrow: for the morrow shall take thought for the things of itself. Sufficient unto the day is the evil thereof." Matthew 6:34.

<u>Prayer:</u> Lord, may I remember that you want me to step out in faith, trusting you to keep me safe for as long as you have work for me to do for you.

293

Have you sometimes found that when you ask people to join you in prayer, they immediately assume that you are stressed and lacking in faith? As it is with normal families, we need to communicate and tell each other the things that are important to us. This is the way we learn about each other and are able to understand how each of us feels about the many issues of life. So, on a spiritual level, one way of communicating with each other, and God, is through prayer requests. So, each time someone asks you to pray for them and a particular situation, remember that God has given you the privilege of getting to know your sister or brother in Christ a little better.

"Praying always with all prayer and supplication in the Spirit, and watching thereunto with all perseverance and supplication for all saints;" Ephesians 6:18.

Prayer: Lord I thank you for the privilege of getting to know my spiritual family through the power of prayer.

294

I understand that, as parents, we hate to see our children hurting. I saw the concern in my father's eyes many times when I was undergoing trials many years ago. Yet each time he voiced his concerns my heart responded with "But I wouldn't change a thing". It wasn't that I enjoyed those trials and if God had given me a choice I would never have said: "Yes, Lord, I will go there for you". Never!

However, through all those times that were difficult and sad, I learned. I learned how to be strong, to use my imagination, to make do with what I had on hand, to use what I had in a different way to solve a problem, and most importantly, I learned to understand others.

Daniel had some friends who were sent into a fire, literally. God's protection was amazing, and God was glorified because of their faith. Now, I'm not going to tell you that I was as faithful as them, but I do believe that God has made me stronger and I have a closer dependence on Him these days.

"That the trial of your faith, being much more precious than of gold that perisheth, though it is tried with fire, might be found unto praise and honour and glory at the appearing of Jesus Christ:" 1 Peter 1:7.

Prayer: Lord, help me to remember that all things precious need to go through fire to be refined.

 295

Thinking about the trails of life, I realized that, if we are in Christ, we are not going to break but be made into something really beautiful. How is a diamond made? In short, it is boiled, in the middle of the earth, thrown out when a volcano erupts, and cooled, yet, it is one of the most valued stones on earth. Even the other rocks and soils that come from the middle of the earth are not as valued as a diamond.

No matter how many trials and struggles we have, we need to remember that God is creating something beautiful and that when it is finished, we will shine for Him with a brilliance that will last for eternity.

"The words of the LORD are pure words; As silver tried in a furnace on the earth, refined seven times." Psalm 12:6 (NAS).

Prayer: Lord, as I struggle through this world, may I remember that You are changing me into something valuable that will bring glory to you.

296

I often get nuisance phone calls from people trying to get me to give them my bank details or private information so they can take my money. They annoy me and make me quite angry. Knowing that this anger was wrong, I worked out a plan to deal with them in a manner that I thought might let them know that what they were doing was really wrong.

I had a great speech about how God could see what they were doing and one day they would have to face Him, and He would not be pleased with them. If they didn't repent, they would get to spend eternity in hell. I'll be honest and tell you that my plan didn't go very well as I still got very angry when I received the next call. I tried to find some compassion, as someone recently said, these people are going to spend a very long time dealing with the fact that they have inflicted so much pain on so many people.

"For we must all appear before the judgment seat of Christ, so that each one may be recompensed for his deeds in the body, according to what he has done, whether good or bad." 2 Corinthians 5:10 (NAS).

Prayer: Lord, help me to tell those who are not your friends, that eternity is a long time to go over all the things that they did wrong.

297

There was a discussion between a family member and myself about something they didn't like. As the discussion continued it turned to things that we often think we want and yet, the reality is usually quite different. The conversation was finished with, "Be careful what you ask for because you may not like what you actually get".

This is often what happens when we put our requests to God. We often ask for something that we believe is good and right, yet, if we were to be given exactly what we asked for, we would find that it really isn't what we wanted at all.

It is a very good thing that God knows better than we do, what is really good for us, and will only give us what that is.

"If you then, being evil, know how to give good gifts to your children, how much more will your Father who is in heaven give what is good to those who ask Him!" Matthew 7:11 (NAS).

Prayer: Lord, may I always remember that you know what is truly best for me, and may I always accept all those gifts from you with the grace with which they are given.

🍷 298

I was really surprised when a young woman declared that women should stop trying so hard to prove that they can do what men can and get on with doing what men can't do.

It's this debate about equality that generates a great deal of emotion and discussion. I have often wondered if, by demanding and getting equal rights, we have actually lost more than we gained. It seems to me that there was a time when the home was considered the domain of the woman. By trying to move into the male domain we have given up some of the authority at home, and yet, kept the responsibility. God has given us very different qualities that make us very different to men.

Of course, that doesn't mean that I believe that women should not work outside the home, but that I believe the work should be carried out in a manner that uses those traits that God has given.

"So, God created man in his own image, in the image of God he created him; male and female he created them." Genesis 1:27.

Prayer: Lord, help me to carry out all the work that you have for me using only the gifts that you have given me rather than in the way I want.

🍷 299

As I continued a discussion with a young woman about the role of women in our world today, it occurred to me that we have distorted, not only the role of women, but also the way that many of the jobs are carried out. As my young friend said, there are very definite reasons why children always want their mothers when they are sick, and why women do the nurturing of people much better than men. This is the way God made us.

Over the years I have often thought that some women have made it much harder for women to get on in the world simply by the way they behave in corporate circles. They do not give us very much credit for being these nurturing creatures God made, simply because they step and stomp over both men and women to get where they want, rather than using their great nurturing skills to work for them and carry them to the top of their field.

Yes, I understand that the lack of respect has driven many before us to take a stand and fight for the rights and privileges that we have today, however, they are being dishonoured as well, by those who take these freedoms to mean that they are able to behave in a rude and crude manner.

> "The wisest of women builds her house, but folly with her own hands tears it down." Proverbs 14:1(ESV).

Prayer: All I want to do, Lord, is bring honour to you.

300

Do you let God sleep in on Monday? It's Sunday and I know that I am going to Church. I prepare myself with a conversation with my Lord. I thank Him for bringing me safely through the week. I worship Him along with the other members sitting in the pews.

Yet, as I listen to the news through the week, I have to wonder how many of those people making headlines, and doing the things that make our lives so hard, were actually sitting in a church somewhere on Sunday? I would like to ask them if they even take God to work with them on Monday. As I pondered this one night, the thought crossed my mind, "Do we let God sleep in on Monday?" Do we ignore what impact He wants to have on our lives and particularly our work situations?

> "Pray without ceasing." 1 Thessalonians 5:17

Prayer: Lord, please come with me every day and help me to consult you in all the decisions I make.

301

As the hot dry weather turns our farm feed to dust, I am becoming very aware that we need another source of income that is not so dependent on the weather. We cannot depend on Government handouts to sustain us forever. I want to be independent. I start asking God about what we can do.

The first response I get is that my book sales are not dependent on weather, so you already have another source. However, Lord, I shoot back, they are not selling enough to make any difference. Everyone knows that you don't make money from writing.

As I was trying to sleep that night, and still thinking about the question, God also nudged me and said "you also have another source of income, one that is very different to dollars and cents, you have to exercise your faith in Me".

"For we walk by faith, not by sight:" 2 Corinthians 5:7

Prayer: Lord, thank you that you know all the things that I need, help me to exercise my faith more and more.

302

A story at church about snakes got me thinking about some of the reasons why humans, in general, don't like them. Maybe it's not just related to the fact that many of them, particularly in Australia, have the ability to kill, or at least make you very sick.

My feeling is that we, rightly or wrongly, associate these creatures with our own sin. Regardless of whether it's correct or not, we associate the snake with the sin of Adam and Eve and, therefore, it is responsible for our sin as well.

I'm sure that, with hindsight, we are all inclined at times to pretend that we would not have been silly enough to give in to the snake's trickery.

We can see all the problems that it caused and, had we been standing where Adam and Eve were, (they didn't have shoes for us to stand in), we would have been just as inclined to do the same thing they did.

Our dislike for snakes, therefore, seems to me to be the same as Adam and Eve's after they were found out. We want to transfer blame to someone or something else, in this case, snakes.

"Wherefore, as by one-man sin entered into the world, and death by sin; and so death passed upon all men, for that all have sinned:" Romans 5:12.

Prayer: Lord, when my pride says that I might not have done something that others have, please remind me that we are all made the same.

303

We all have legendary family stories that we often bring out to tell at family gatherings. In our family, it's my health as a baby, and my brother's reaction to my father's treatment of a wild pig when he was around one year old. For us, it's my daughter's reaction to a snake, and my son's comments about heaven that gets told time and time again. These stories are all true and cute even if they become stretched a little over time.

There is, of course, one story that is also true, but not cute, and that is the story of God's provision of salvation for the human race. It's a story that should be told again and again, but I suspect that sometimes we are not that keen to repeat it as many times as we would like to tell the family ones.

"And thou shalt teach them diligently unto thy children, and shalt talk of them when thou sittest in thine house, and when thou walkest by the way, and when thou liest down, and when thou risest up." Deuteronomy 6:7.

Prayer: Lord, help me to tell your wonderful story of salvation over, and over again, to bring honour to your name.

 304

I often ask parents how their children are, and surprisingly, the answer I often get is: "I don't know, I only hear from them when they want something, or when there is something wrong". What these family members don't realise is that, if they expect their parents to be there in the bad, they really should continue to relate to them during the good times as well. It really would be appreciated by parents.

I continued to think about us as humans in general. Too often, we expect God to be there when things go wrong yet, when the good times are happening, how often do we push God into the background of our lives?

God wants to have a relationship with us during the good times as well as the bad times. He wants us to learn lessons from the good things that happen to us as well as the tough times.

"Rejoice always; pray without ceasing; in everything give thanks; for this is God's will for you in Christ Jesus." 1 Thessalonians 5:16-18 (NAS).

Prayer: Lord, help me to remember to praise you for the good things, and not just ask for your help when things get tough.

305

I had a tough week and, as always, I was inclined to complain a lot about the issues that I was dealing with. One morning I was thinking and praying for a family who was dealing with the death of a family member, and trying to cope with ill family members at the same time. God tapped me on the shoulder and I realized that I really was very blessed. I apologised to God once again for being such a grumbler.

There are so many people out there that have greater problems than I am dealing with, and yet these people continue to grow in their faith. It was then that I realized that they continue to grow because they are having to exercise their faith muscles all the time.

We only get fitter if we continue to exercise our bodies. We have all seen the stories of elite athletes who struggle to stay fit after they retire from their sporting careers. The same thing could happen to us spiritually, not because we have retired, but because we have stopped stretching ourselves spiritually.

"Wherefore seeing we also are compassed about with so great a cloud of witnesses, let us lay aside every weight and the sin which doth so easily beset *us*, and let us run with patience the race that is set before us,"
Hebrews 12:1.

Prayer: May I always exercise my faith muscles in order to bring glory to you.

306

I was thinking about the many people that I know who face so many problems day after day, week after week, year after year, and yet these people are not broken, they are strong witnesses for their Lord. How do they stay so spiritually fit Lord? I asked, as I debated this in my head.

"They are strong because they have to exercise their faith muscles all the time. They have to depend on me all the time for their strength".

We have heard so many stories about people who have worked very hard over an extended period of time to lose weight, or got very fit, and then suffered an illness or injury and slipped rapidly into their previous unhealthy condition. This has happened because they have been unable to keep up their regime.

We only gain spiritual strength by continuing to exercise our faith muscles every minute of the day. I was about to ask God to give me this strength when I stopped myself. You might ask why I stopped myself? Well, the reason is this. If I am going to ask for that strength, it will mean that I will be faced with many more problems and issues that I am not sure I want to face right now.

Can I gain spiritual strength without extra problems and issues that force me to depend on our God? I think probably not. This is why James tells us to be thankful for the trials and tribulations that come our way because they are the spiritual weights that allow us to get spiritually fit.

"My brethren, count it all joy when ye fall into divers temptations; Knowing *this*, that the trying of your faith worketh patience. But let patience have *her* perfect work, that ye may be perfect and entire, wanting nothing." James 1:2-4.

Prayer: Lord, give me the courage to gain more strength.

 # 307

There are so many things that take the romance out of love. It could be things such as illness, sleep deprivation, dealing with drought, or many other issues. As I see it, the truth is that, while these things can take the romance out, they do not destroy the love that we have. I have heard some people tell me that love is ninety-nine percent hard work.

There are so many people that will tell us that, without romance, there is no love and that is why you see people falling out of love, often many times over. Love is not just made up of romance, it's also made up of loyalty, patience, commitment, and perseverance. It is also a choice that we make. There was nothing romantic about the cross, but Jesus still went there out of love for you and me.

"For this reason, the Father loves me because I lay down my life that I may take it up again. No one takes it from me, but I lay it down of my own accord. I have authority to lay it down, and I have authority to take it up again. This charge I have received from my Father." John 10:17-18 (ESV).

Prayer: Thank you, Lord, for loving me so much that you did this for me.

308

Have you ever had trouble recognising people out of context? By that I mean, you know that you should know that person, but because they are not where you would normally see them, you cannot place them. I had this happen to me one day at a funeral. There were a couple of people who attended and I was sure that I should know them. It wasn't until I was told, or worked out where they worked, that I realized who they were.

This got me thinking later about recognising people when we get to Heaven. Will we know them instantly or will it take time to place them? I thought about a dream one person had about their late spouse, they looked exactly as they did on earth but they had a perfect complexion. It's hard to know for sure what life will be like in Heaven, but then, that's what faith is all about, isn't it?

"Now faith is the substance of things hoped for, the evidence of things not seen." Hebrews 11:1.

Prayer: Lord, may I have confidence that whatever lies beyond the grave will be beautiful.

🍷 309

It was another day of long to-do lists and interruptions which meant that I was going to forget to do something if I wasn't careful. As I returned to the house after another "extra" job, I prayed: "Lord, you are the God of time, and therefore, you are the creator of my timetable. Please help me to do, and get to, things on time, I hand control over to you".

This was the only way I was going to get through the day. I knew from previous experience that if I tried to rush around in a panic, I would end up messing up badly. This is something that I had to learn when I had five children at home and at one stage had them in five different schools.

"And He said to His disciples, "For this reason, I say to you, do not worry about *your* life, *as to* what you will eat; nor for your body, *as to* what you will put on........... "But if God so clothes the grass in the field, which is *alive* today and tomorrow is thrown into the furnace, how much more *will He clothe* you? You men of little faith!" Luke 12:22,28 (NAS).

<u>**Prayer:**</u> Lord, I thank you for keeping me calm and allowing me to get all those important things done.

🍷 310

I woke in the early hours of the morning and wondered what time it was. I listened for the noises around me. If the chooks were crowing, then I figured that it would be about four thirty. I turned the light on to check the time and it was already five o'clock. "Wow, why are the chooks not up yet?"

I realized then that the chooks were adjusting to the change in the seasons, it was now Autumn and they were sleeping longer, just as the nights were getting longer.

I am getting older, my season is changing, I am heading, well and truly, into my Autumn years (or is it Winter) and yet I still struggle with the adjustments that I have to make. Tiredness is the one I hate the most, not being able to run all day flat out and still have energy left over.

Yet, God wants me to enjoy this time of my life, and I can only do that if I make the adjustments that are necessary and the biggest one is to be thankful, after all, there are still many things that I CAN do.

"In everything give thanks: for this is the will of God in Christ Jesus concerning you." 1 Thessalonians 5:18.

Prayer: Lord, I thank you that, while life changes, you don't.

311

The bread had been thawing out for a while now, but I needed to use it for morning tea. As I started to separate the slices, I discovered that the bread was still frozen in the middle. Prying the slices apart, I had to tell myself to be very careful, or I would render the bread useless.

As I was spreading the butter, another thought occurred to me. Aren't we just like that bread, frozen in the middle? No matter how long we have been walking with the Lord, there will always be things in our lives that have to be dealt with, improved on, and thawed out. Yet, our Lord needs to use us to spread His word and love.

He gently separates us from the loaf, sends us out into the world to work for Him. He leads us with a gentle hand even if we feel that we are still stuck in our past.

"For it is God which worketh in you both to will and to do of _his_ good pleasure." Philippians 2:13.

Prayer: Lord, use me regardless of what still has to be fixed inside of me.

312

Listening to the sounds around us is sometimes a good way to work out what might be happening outside. If the dogs are barking, then there could be an intruder, a fox, a wild pig, or just sheep getting too close to their territory. The chooks will make different noises that tell us that something is wrong, an egg has been laid, or it's just early morning.

Listening to what God has to tell us in His word is also a good way to work out what is happening in our lives. It helps us to understand what is wrong with us, and why we feel the way we do about certain things, and best of all, it tells us how to fix it.

"All scripture *is* given by inspiration of God, and *is* profitable for doctrine, for reproof, for correction, for instruction in righteousness:" 2 Timothy 3:16

Prayer: Lord, give me ears to hear your warnings and instructions.

313

Early one morning, as I checked the clock to see what time it was, I realized that we are always checking things. We watch the weather report or the sky to check on the weather, we check our Facebook to see what our friends are doing, we listen to the news to see what is happening around the world. Checking is not a bad thing, it's just that sometimes what we are told is not always entirely truthful.

We not only do this checking to learn what has happened, but to try and work out what might happen in the future. If there are certain clouds in the sky, we try to work out if there is just rain coming or if they mean there is an approaching storm, a barking dog alerts us to be prepared for something or someone that could be approaching. Sometimes what we think might be going to happen may not be as bad as we thought, and sometimes doesn't happen at all. We humans are very good at getting things wrong, aren't we?

We only have to read our Bibles to see how the people who lived while Jesus was here on earth also got so many things mixed up and I'm afraid we are not so very different to them.

"For there is no partiality with God." Romans 2:11 (NAS).

Prayer: Lord, please teach me that, flawed as we are, your grace extends to all of us equally.

314

The Bible is God's word and, if we listen to what He has to say, we will hear lots about the future and all of it is true. So, we need to check out our Bibles every day to find out where we have gone wrong in the past, how He can help us now, and what our future holds.

Just like the weatherman, many people try and tell us what might happen, and yet, only God knows for sure how things are really going to play out. We cannot see the future and, because we are human, we can read things the wrong way. How many times have we looked at the dark clouds in the sky and thought we were going to get rain, and none has fallen, or looked at a storm that never arrives?

What God wants us to do is deal with the here and now, trust Him for the future and, when He is ready, He will reveal everything that we need to know. If it is worse than we thought, He will be there to help us through it. If it is better than we predicted, then we need to thank Him for His blessings.

"All scripture _is_ given by inspiration of God, and _is_ profitable for doctrine, for reproof, for correction, for instruction in righteousness:" 2 Timothy 3:16

Prayer: Lord, your word is absolutely true, so please help me to apply it to me first.

🍷 315

During a phone call to a friend, they mentioned that they had surgery and this meant that they were unable to do many of the things that they wanted to carry out. As I prayed for them, I thought about how we don't realize how much we use a particular part of our body until it is out of action.

Each part of our bodies is very important, God put it there for a particular purpose. It doesn't mean that we cannot live without certain parts. Some of God's greatest warriors have had to cope with major physical challenges. Paul is just one example of a very long list.

We are all part of God's church and not one of us will be spiritually perfect, yet our Lord and God will use us, if only we will allow Him to work through us.

"And he said unto me, My grace is sufficient for thee: for my strength is made perfect in weakness. Most gladly, therefore, will I rather glory in my infirmities, that the power of Christ may rest upon me." 2 Corinthians 12:9.

Prayer: Lord, may I be used for you, just the way I am.

🍷 316

As I prepared to write one morning, I found myself hunting around for several chargers. I needed one for the internet, one for the computer, and one for my mobile phone. While I was hunting around, I was telling myself that life would be much easier if I didn't need these things and/or I could remember where I had used them last. It seems that some days, I spend as much time getting ready as I do actually carrying out a task.

However, that is what our life is all about. We are here on earth, preparing ourselves for eternity. If we live according to the way God intended, in a relationship with Jesus, then we get to spend eternity in Heaven. If, however, we spend it doing what we want, ignoring Christ's gift of salvation, then Hell is our destination.

"So, shall it be at the end of the world: the angels shall come forth, and sever the wicked from among the just," Matthew 13:49.

Prayer: Lord, may my preparations for eternity be carried out with diligence.

317

I was watching a couple of TV programs on the restoration and the history of two very different houses. The presenters did some amazing research to find out about all the people that had worked, lived, loved, and died in them over the previous 100 years. I thought about all the changes that had taken place, and how many people had their dreams shattered, fulfilled, and changed. I marvelled at how the presenters were able to find out so much about the people that had lived so long ago.

I was once asked about who I would most like to talk to when I reached Heaven, and while I gave a short answer then, the real answer is that I want to talk to everyone that is there. I want to hear about the things we were never told. You see the problem is that we can never record everything that happens. While the earthly things will no longer be important, I still think they will be of interest.

"And there are also many other things which Jesus did, the which, if they should be written every one, I suppose that even the world itself could not contain the books that should be written. Amen." John 21:25.

Prayer: Lord, help me to remember the good things, and learn from the difficult things.

318

I was humbled as a young Christian woman and I discussed the decisions that she had made during a time of ill health. She had decided not to wait until her health improved to do the things that she wanted to do. Had she waited, she would never have gotten married, had any children, started her own business, or anything else, so she had made a deliberate decision to live her life the way she wanted to, despite her health.

As I continued to think about this young woman, I realized just how sensible she was, and how silly it was of me to expect her to get her health sorted first. So many people will tell you that they will look after their spiritual issues when they have more time, or when they have their business sorted, after they have become better people, or any number of other reasons, yet, we know that they need to come to Jesus now, and deal with it now, because they never know when God will call them home. Jesus wants us to come to Him today, He doesn't want us to wait until later, He will help us to live for Him regardless of the state of our spiritual health. He doesn't want us to wait, He wants us to get on with life and live it for Him.

"...behold, now *is* the accepted time; behold, now *is* the day of salvation."
2 Corinthians 6:2b.

Prayer: Lord, help me to move forward regardless of the many obstacles I think may be in front of me.

319

    Life is such a rollercoaster ride for those of us who are fortunate enough to have children. One moment, you're proud as can be, the next, terrified by what they are doing, and then there are those moments when your heart is breaking because there is nothing harder for a parent, than to stand by and watch their child go through great pain. If there is only one child, it's tough, but add a few siblings and the ride gets quite a bit faster as each child puts you through a different corner all at once.

    It was one of those mornings when all my children had given me something different to work through. As I prayed for each one of them, knowing that I had failed to communicate effectively to any of them, I realized that God has a much bigger workload. He is watching all His children and He not only sees all, but overhears what they are thinking as well. Oh, boy, am I glad I do not have the power to read people's minds.

    Still, He is the perfect parent, He knows what is best for each one of us, He also has the power to meet our needs at the right time, in the right way, and for the right reasons. All we have to do is trust Him and wait, and that is another scary ride in itself sometimes.

"If ye then, being evil, know how to give good gifts unto your children, how much more shall your Father which is in heaven give good things to them that ask him?" Matthew 7:11.

Prayer: Lord, thank you for being my perfect, loving Father.

320

    The mosquitoes swarmed around the bathroom and each time I moved something, I disturbed another cloud of them, sending them spinning into the air. I inwardly complained to God about these nasty creatures to the point where I even suggested that God didn't create them, or that they had been converted from having some good purpose into evil creatures of mass annoyance.

Out came the bug spray and I effectively disposed of most of them, leaving their dead bodies all over the white surfaces of my bathroom. The next morning, as I cleaned up their scattered remains, I was again wondering how I could be thankful for such animals.

As I turned on the water, God nudged me, reminding me that that many mosquitoes means that somewhere there is water. They cannot breed or live without it, so, even though your paddocks are dry and the grass is dying, there is water somewhere. Just like some of my good gifts, they are not always visible to you in the here and now. They are around you but you cannot always see them, I could be storing them up for a future blessing.

> **"For I know the thoughts that I think toward you, saith the LORD, thoughts of peace, and not of evil, to give you an expected end."**
> **Jeremiah 29:11**

Prayer: Lord, forgive me for not seeing your blessings in the unpleasant things around me.

321

Maybe it's as a result of our large open spaces in Australia, but I am often discouraged by the number of human leaders who think that the only way to get people to do things is to drive them. Here in Australia, we round up our stock from the rear, pushing them forwards into a new paddock or yards, onto trucks, or into sheds. It has always been done this way from our very early days of settlement.

When things are tough and we have to hand feed sheep, the fastest way to get an animal to go anywhere is to put feed out. They will come running even to the point of exhaustion. I have no idea how it is done in eastern countries today, but when Jesus walked on this earth it was a matter of leading sheep.

So, if you are a leader, and you want people to go somewhere different, here is a small piece of advice (and I don't give it very often) – Lead! Lead by example, lead from the front. It doesn't matter if you are a leader of a small church, an organisation, a town, a state, or the country. Show the people that you love them so much that you will be willing to give up your life for them. Jesus said in John 10:11

> **"I am the good shepherd: the good shepherd giveth his life for the sheep."**

Follow the best leader and be a great leader yourself.

Prayer: Lord, thank you for being a gentle leader so that I may follow you faithfully.

322

My father has often said that you cannot improve the future without disturbing the present. I have to say though, that I really don't like the present being disturbed too much. This was brought home to me during a time when we were renovating our laundry. I was very excited to start with, finally, my laundry was going to be finished! I had only been waiting fifteen years or so for it to happen, Yah! However, as the process took longer than I anticipated, I found my excitement dwindling somewhat as my verandas continued to be a mess, and there was dust over everything for weeks. I really had to pray for patience!

Yet, as I thought about it, there was a present time which was really disturbed, two thousand years ago, to improve our future. As I understand it, there were some people back then that didn't like it at all. Jesus said a lot of things that disturbed the Roman and church leaders and they didn't like that one bit.

Even now, when we accept Jesus into our lives, there is a great disturbance that happens, we have to change the way we live and deal with those sins in our lives that He does not want there but our futures are assured and will be totally undisturbed.

> "Think not that I am come to send peace on earth: I came not to send peace, but a sword." Matthew 10:34.

Prayer: Lord, I thank you that life in Heaven will never have to be disturbed to be improved, ever!

323

When we have to wait a long time for something to happen, our perception about how things will turn out can often be very different to the reality. I had this problem when we started renovating our home. It was all supposed to happen quickly and without disturbing the family routine too much. The actuality, of course, was completely different. Twenty years on and we still have not finished the job. I was thinking about this one morning, and realized that I wasn't that different to the people who lived in Israel two thousand years ago.

On Palm Sunday, the people were very excited about the arrival of their new king, He was riding on a donkey just as the prophets had predicted. Their salvation was at hand; it was finally going to happen.

Yet, a week later, progress hadn't been made, the job wasn't done, the Romans were still in power. Why were things taking so long!? Like me, their perception of how things would unfold was off. He knew what was going to happen, and He had told the people hundreds of years before what was going to happen, yet they could not envisage how it was actually going to work out.

I'm sure that many of us are the same when we come to Jesus, we have plans and ideas about how He will work in our lives, which sins He will clean up first, and we are often puzzled when He does something completely different but one thing is for certain, it will be done, it has been done, and some day we will see the whole plan completed.

"For Christ also hath once suffered for sins, the just for the unjust, that he might bring us to God, being put to death in the flesh, but quickened by the Spirit:" 1 Peter 3:18

Prayer: Lord Jesus, I thank you that what you have done for me is enough to bring me into the fellowship of my Heavenly Father.

324

Where might we find the greatest set of instructions we can ever have in life? Yes, the Bible. The Bible, however, cannot be called a macro set of instructions, because the bible doesn't give us anything in an abbreviated format. There are instructions and principals written in this, the greatest book of all time, but they are still definitely written in full. How we apply the principals to our everyday lives will be different to those in other circumstances, places, and times, but the principals are very clear. There would be some people who would insist on the instructions being applied to the letter of the law, without the grace of God being applied at all. This sadly creates more problems than it solves.

"For sin shall not have dominion over you: for ye are not under the law, but under grace." Romans 6:14

The bible tells us in 2 Timothy 3:16:

"All scripture *is* given by inspiration of God, and *is* profitable for doctrine, for reproof, for correction, for instruction in righteousness:"

Challenge: Let us read the instructions and principals and apply them to our lives with the grace of God that extends love to us, and therefore, allows us to be channels of love and blessing to those around us.

325

I was praying early one morning, and I got off track. I speculated about what I would say if a boss who had a high turnover of staff asked me how to fix the problem. My first response would be that he would need to get rid of the bullies in the organisation. Of course, he was going to ask me how that could possibly be done. After all, you cannot sack too many people at once, otherwise the business would fail to function at all. To cure a bully, they must change from the inside out, they cannot be forced to change by rules, regulations, or teaching, they must make the choice to change their behaviour themselves. Yes, it goes without saying that, once they make that choice, we can assist, but nothing can be done until the choice is made in the first place.

So, how then is a boss supposed to affect such changes in his workplace? My suggestion was that he needs to pray for each member of staff first thing each day and leave the rest up to the Lord. That's is when I realized that every boss and leader in the world has a very large congregation to minister to. It is not just the responsibility of the church to witness to the world, but the obligation of each and every person who has authority over others.

"And, ye masters, do the same things unto them, forbearing *(stop)* threatening: knowing that your Master also is in heaven; neither is there respect of persons with him." Ephesians 6:9.

Prayer: Lord, you have given me many people to witness to, may I carry it out faithfully.

326

It was early morning and I wanted to get some gardening done before it got too hot. Normally, I am a careful weeder, finding the root of the weed and pulling it out carefully in order to not disturb the plants around it. On this occasion, however, I was in a grab and pull mood. As I threw the stuff in the wheelbarrow, I could see good plants. I knew that they might, given the right conditions, take root and flourish in the places where I was about to throw them.

It reminded me of the church in Jerusalem in the first century, how it was apparently being damaged, but it was God's plan to spread His word to other parts of the world.

Isn't it much the same today? God's church is under pressure and yet, God is still faithfully looking after all His children.

"And the LORD, he *it is* that doth go before thee; he will be with thee, he will not fail thee, neither forsake thee: fear not, neither be dismayed." Deuteronomy 31:8.

Prayer: Lord, thank you for going before me wherever you lead.

327

What question do you think God gets asked the most? I have a feeling that it is "why?" We ask it so many times. Yet, without it, there would not have been any progress in this world. I seem to remember being told that James Watt was able to eventually invent the steam engine by asking the question about why steam lifted the lid on a kettle. Asking why sometimes takes us to the next step in our progress.

There are times, however, when it just creates a barrier that hinders our progress, we just need to trust God to work things out and wait to see how He answers us in the future.

"I press toward the mark for the prize of the high calling of God in Christ Jesus." Philippians 3:14.

Prayer: Lord, may I be given the wisdom to know when to ask "why?" and when to trust you.

♟ 328

The future stretched out in front of me, long and boring. It wasn't even that it was an enforced confinement, I just had nowhere to go. It wasn't that I had no dreams to reach for, I wanted to spread my wings, but at each turn, I found there was no way of making it happen. Sometimes it was a lack of opportunity, other times, a lack of courage or other, more important priorities, that kept me grounded.

I thought about Paul being a prisoner. My heart told me that he would have had many visitors to keep him in contact with people, but my head told me that there would have been many hours, days, and even weeks when he would not have seen a soul. Paul learned to be content with what God asked of him, and so must I.

"I know both how to be abased, and I know how to abound: everywhere and in all things, I am instructed both to be full and to be hungry, both to abound and to suffer need." Philippians 4:12.

Prayer: May I be content with what you have given me because Lord, you have given me so much to be grateful for.

329

As I thought about what I wanted to do and what I was realizing that God wanted me to do, I had to think about how Jesus battled with the price He was going to pay for my sins on the cross.

"Saying, Father, if thou be willing, remove this cup from me: nevertheless, not my will, but thine, be done." Luke 22:42.

Yet, He loved me enough to complete my redemption and that of everyone who has ever sinned and accepts that gift of grace.

"In Him, we have redemption through His blood, the forgiveness of our trespasses, according to the riches of His grace" Ephesians 1:7.

Prayer: Lord, I cannot imagine the pain that my sins have cost you, but I accept the gift of grace you have given to me.

330

These days many people try to tell us that "Mother Nature" is responsible for controlling the weather and seasons. However, God made them all and we should honour Him even when the weather brings problems to deal with such as droughts, storms, and floods.

It is His inspiration that enables us to work out how to live within the boundaries of the weather, to heat or cool our homes, and to develop plants that grow within the confines of short summers or very cold winters.

"Neither say they in their heart, Let us now fear the LORD our God, that giveth rain, both the former and the latter, in his season: he preserveth unto us the appointed weeks of the harvest." Jeremiah 5:24.

Prayer: To God be the glory for it is He who controls the weather.

331

I think birthdays are our own personal Thanksgiving Day, a day when we look back over the past year and forward at the next. As I wrote my Christmas Letter last night, I was able to share just how much I have to be thankful for. Looking back over this last year I can see that the hand of God moved me to do exactly what needed, because He knew what was going to happen. I can now see, that even in the midst of the down times, and I don't just mean the passing of my mother, (there was a lot of time in the middle of the year where I really questioned what God's plan was for the year and even the rest of my life), His hand was working.

As I spoke to my dad this morning, I commented that modern media is a two-edged sword. It raises the expectations of people too high and this will impact on their optimism. For the first time, I have some idea of what the next year holds, so many firsts without my mother but at the same time: Jeremiah 29:11 says:

"For I know the thoughts that I think toward you, saith the Lord, thoughts of peace and not of evil, to give you an expected end"

The year ahead is under God's control.

Prayer: Lord, thank you for everything.

332

God's spiritual training exercises are not easy. He wants us to participate in them so that we can strengthen our spiritual muscles. If we don't hold his hand while we are doing them, we will find them to be overwhelming and they will break us. If we hold His hand, we will not only triumph, we will help others along the way, and we will be made fitter for his kingdom.

"For bodily exercise profiteth little: but godliness is profitable unto all things, having the promise of the life that now is, and of that which is to come." 1 Timothy 4:8

Challenge: Trust God that what He allows, will make us stronger, not break us.

 333

When you become a mother, you get what my father calls "mother's ears". Before you get "mother's ears" you might very well have slept through a thunderstorm, but now when a child coughs, or makes the slightest noise, you instantly wake up and even if you don't get up, you listen carefully to make sure that they are alright. This happens because our brains know that we are responsible for looking after these children, and so it tunes into them, and wakes us up as soon as it hears something.

As I was thinking about this early one morning, I was wondering how many of us have "faith ears" switched on? God does not always speak to us in a loud voice. He, more often than not, will speak to us in the softest of ways, so we have to tune our souls, with the help of the Holy Spirit, to listen to what God wants us to hear with our "faith ears".

"And after the earthquake, there was a fire, but the LORD was not in the fire. And after the fire, there was the sound of a gentle whisper." 1 Kings 19:12.

Prayer: Lord, may I always listen to you with my "faith ears".

334

I was woken, very early, in the dark by a noise that told me that a rodent was in my room somewhere. I am not particularly fond of these creatures. ,In order to stop it running around my room, I turned on my bedside light and went back to sleep.

No, I am not afraid of the dark, but I know that rodents are afraid of the light, and therefore, would have gone back into hiding.

Many people are also afraid of the light! The light of God which shows us our faults, our sins, and how much we need saving from the darkness of evil.

It was God, who said,

"Let light shine out of darkness," has shone in our hearts to give the light of the knowledge of the glory of God in the face of Jesus Christ. 2 Corinthians 4:6

Prayer: Lord, let you light continue to shine in my life no matter how uncomfortable that might make me feel.

335

I spent some time in my garden during a drought. I had been neglecting it as it seemed to be a pointless exercise. There was no rain to make my work worthwhile. As I was cleaning up, I had a thought: dead or alive my garden needs to be cared for. So, the thought that followed was; the world, dead or alive, needs to be cared for as well.

Is this how some Christians see our world? So dead that it is beyond help, in so much trouble that the job is way too big? God cares for us anyway!

> "Do you not say, 'There are yet four months, then comes the harvest'? Look, I tell you, lift up your eyes, and see that the fields are white for harvest." John 4:35

Prayer: Lord, help me not to stop working for you, no matter how big the workload looks.

336

I lay awake one morning at 2 am and my imagination went on a bender. I was thinking about what would happen if God decided to dispose of those satellites floating out there in space.

There would be no internet service, and we would suddenly find ourselves very isolated. Now, I know what you are thinking, this is impossible, it's just not going to happen, BUT, our God allowed us to develop all this technology and He is way ahead of us in where it is going and how it is going to affect our lives. What He allows, He can also take from us.

I look around our world and think that we, as a society, are so arrogant and I wonder if we have not reached the same level as those who were around during the time of Babel. If the internet was to drop out, we would have to slow down, take more effort and..... well who knows what good things might come of it, along with the bad, sad, and ugly.

So yes, while I doubt my own imagination, I wonder if it will take something like this to bring us all back to depending on Him.

Job knew this truth

> "He said, "Naked I came out of my mother's womb, and naked will I return there. Yahweh gave, and Yahweh has taken away. Blessed be Yahweh's name." Job 1:21

Prayer: Lord, help me to depend on You first, and your gifts, second.

337

I have lit the wood stove in the middle of summer. Why? Thunderstorms are a big part of our Australian summers and often, when they get wound up, our electricity gets cut off. The wood stove allows us to indulge in a hot meal and hot drinks while we wait for those poor workers, suffering in stormy weather, to reconnect us.

I have been advised, on many occasions, to dispose of our wonderful pieces of history and go all electric. I refused! I wanted to keep our fuel stove, as well as our high tank, which gravity feeds water to the taps. This amazing high tank watering system is currently out of action as the tank has developed a hole, which gravity feeds water straight out onto the ground. This means that we are currently dependent on electricity to make sure that our house has a constant water flow. But the wood stove is still functioning. It still cooks a decent meal, and boils water hotter than the electric jug, so I rejoice in that much.

As our technology advances and gets more elaborate, it will be harder to hang onto what is considered old fashioned technology. I see no need to dispose of such equipment; it works effectively and is really much greener than people give it credit for.

"Yahweh preserves the simple. I was brought low, and he saved me."
Psalm 116:6

There is a saying that goes along the lines of "it's not wise to put all your eggs in the one basket", and I would agree. This is my effort at doing just that.

<u>**Challenge:**</u> Remember, God's imagination is so much bigger than ours.

338

One of the problems I have with sitting comfortably in front of the heater during winter is that I find it hard to move. I watch the wood burn down. I know that I have to get up and put more wood on it to keep it burning properly and I just don't feel like going out into the cold bleak weather to fetch the wood.

I have to wonder if that is a problem that many Christians face. Are they just so comfortable in the way they are living that they don't want to face the cruel, sad world of sin outside their church life?

**"And the master said to the servant, 'Go out into the highways and hedges and compel people to come in, that my house may be filled."
Luke 14:23.**

It's not comfortable out there in the real world but that is where the Lord wants us to be.

Prayer: Lord, please help me to walk out into the real world instead of staying comfortable in front of my heater.

339

As teenagers, we are so self-conscious. We think that when we mess up, the whole world will see, criticise us, and remember it forever. Yet, when we grow up, we realize that most of our peers were too busy worrying about their own gaffs, to even notice ours, let alone remember them.

Fast forward to the end of time. The whole of existence will be gathered before the God of creation. Do we think that they will all care about our sins? I don't think so. I think they will be too concerned with their own status, to worry about anyone else.

"And I saw the dead, great and small, standing before the throne, and books were opened. Then another book was opened, which is the book of life. And the dead were judged by what was written in the books, according to what they had done." Revelation 20:12.

Prayer: Lord, may I only be concerned about what you think of me because most people won't even remember me.

🍷 340

There was a point in my life in which my future looked a little foggy. I could only see a very little way in front of me. The rest of the road seemed covered in the fog of uncertainty. There were so many things that I would have liked to do, and life was just difficult. When I managed to do some things, I found myself so tired afterward that I wondered if I would ever have enough energy to do anything I wanted to do.

I was given a gift that says, "Dreams don't work unless you do." I am certain that I am not the only person who has stood at the point that I was standing at. In order to move forward, we need faith. I must hold the hand of my Lord and move forward.

"Now faith is confidence in what we hope for and assurance about what we do not see." Hebrews 11:1 (NIV) so ".... we walk by faith, not by sight:" 2 Corinthians 5:7

One thing I am certain of, and can clearly see in my mind's eye, is that one day I will be standing in front of the throne of God

"And as it is appointed unto men once to die, but after this the judgment:" Hebrews 9:27.

With that look of love, He will say, "welcome my child, you worked hard for me" and I will bow my head in shame and say, "but Lord, I did complain a lot".

Prayer: Lord, help me to work in whatever the circumstances without complaining anymore.

341

In Australia, we used to have only one authority which was responsible for our telephone services. Then, one day, those in charge decided that competition would be a very good idea. Yes, it meant that there were cheaper deals available, but it also meant that when it came to fixing problems and faults, a lot of people had to talk to a lot of other people in order to achieve a good outcome.

I was discussing this with my father, who had had problems with his phone service for a couple of weeks and he declared; 'It's a good thing that there are no such problems with the line to God, it's always open and working'.

How true this is! Our calls to God will never drop out, never be affected by stormy weather, or someone pushing the wrong button on a computer. The only way that this line will not work, is if we, as humans, stop talking to our Heavenly Father.

"But **verily God hath heard** *me;* **he hath attended to the voice of my prayer. Blessed** *be* **God, which hath not turned away my prayer, nor his mercy from me." Psalm 66:19-20.**

Challenge: May I always keep the line open to my Lord, by always talking to Him about matters, large and small.

342

I was in pain; I coped with it for a couple of days by using painkillers and heat packs. Suddenly, I had relief. It was then that I realized that the pain that I felt was what we call referred pain. It turned out to be a pinched nerve, but, while I felt the pain in my head, the nerve was caught down in my shoulder. Relief came when I moved, releasing the nerve. For a couple of days afterward I would feel twinges but what I noticed was that my hand always went to where the pain was felt, not to where the problem was.

On a spiritual level, we tend to do the same thing. We try to solve the wrong where we see the problem, not at its source. For instance, we enforce new laws rather than trying to work out what drives people to do the wrong thing in the first place.

Yes, I know that the sinful nature will always be the root of the problem, but there are other reasons why people turn to unruly behaviour. They may be bored, desperate or ill among other things. These are the things that must be treated first, in order to create a better society.

"And let us not be weary in well doing: for in due season we shall reap, if we faint not". Galatians 6:9.

Prayer: Oh Lord, please show me where the real problem is when I meet those you want me to help.

343

In the early days of our life on the farm, I was very keen to place my stamp on the place, particularly in the garden. I love roses and, as far as I'm concerned, no garden is complete without some.

However, like that saying about some people going where even angels fear to tread, I bought some roses and planted them. A couple of years later, I decided that they really shouldn't be in that particular spot and so I had my husband move them. Well, they both died, and I now have a problem trying to get rid of the rootstock that keeps coming up.

I thought about those roses and how they relate to us sometimes. God plants us in a particular spot for His purposes. There will be problems to deal with, and the situation might not be ideal, but God has put us there. Unlike me and the roses, God won't uproot us and shift us somewhere else just because the position isn't perfect. He will give us the strength to stay planted where we are and work for Him.

"But he answered and said, Every plant, which my heavenly Father hath not planted, shall be rooted up." Matthew 15:13.

Challenge: Lord, help me to remember that you have put me here for your purpose and I will flourish under your care.

344

On a cold morning, I was sitting in front of my heater. It was going, but not giving out as much heat as I would have liked. It had two logs in it but they were burning separately. They should have been providing a lot of heat for the house, so, I opened the door and pushed them together and surprise, surprise they started to burn faster and hotter.

It reminded me of the verse Hebrews 10:25

"Not forsaking the assembling of ourselves together, as the manner of some *is*; but exhorting *one another*: and so much the more, as ye see the day approaching."

We burn better, faster, and therefore, make a greater difference when we work together with those who have similar passions and goals.

Prayer: Lord, please show me who you want me to work with today to spread your message around the world.

🍷 345

It's winter again, and the job of collecting wood for our heater is part of our routine once again. When filling the wood box, it is important to make sure that it contains not only large night logs, but also smaller pieces. This is to ensure that the larger logs burn efficiently instead of just smouldering.

As I collected smaller logs one day, I thought about how our roles in life can be similar to the various logs in my wood box.

Some of us feel as if the jobs God has given us are small and insignificant. We might be right. We might be like those smaller logs that I put on my fire. Our job is to support those with the larger jobs in life. We are to provide air and support that enables them to burn very brightly and do the larger work of spreading the gospel to the world. Without our faithful service, these people would just smoulder and their work would be so much harder.

When speaking to the crowd that wanted to complicate His ministry with rules and regulations we find that Jesus told them,

"This is the only work God wants from you: Believe in the one he has sent." John 6:29.

It sounds like such a small thing but, do this faithfully, and God's work will burn with a force that the world will never be able to stop.

Prayer: Lord, may I be faithful in the small things, so the larger things are made easier for those to whom you have given the greater responsibility.

🍷 346

I was woken through the night by the dogs constant barking making it impossible for me to sleep. I thought about how some people are kept awake by worries and fear. They are just as effective as those dogs barking outside my window.

In order to stop my dogs barking, I would have to actually get out of bed and find out what they were barking at and eliminate it. However, sometimes they bark at imaginary shadows, just like we sometimes worry about imaginary things. The solution to stop the worries and fears that keep us awake can be found in 1 Peter 5:7,

"Casting all your care upon him; for He careth for you."

Challenge: When the dogs bark in my head, Lord, help me to remember that you are waiting to take care of them.

347

There is a sleepy little town that I drive through quite often. It is always quiet, and it appears that not a lot happens. I recently met some Christians who had been called to live there and wondered why God would ask these people to live in such a town. Yet, as I got to know these wonderful Christians, I discovered that there was a lot of spiritual activity going on, that you just didn't see while driving through.

I realized that the same thing happens with the people we meet. They may seem to be quiet and not doing a lot for the Lord, but maybe there is a lot happening that we just don't see.

In 1 Samuel 16:7 we read,

"But the Lord said unto Samuel, Look not on his countenance, or on the height of his stature; because I have refused him: for the Lord seeth not as man seeth; for man looketh on the outward appearance, but the Lord looketh on the heart."

Prayer: Lord, help me not to judge people by what I see.

♆ 348

Wattle trees, as far as I know, grow only in Australia. They have grey-green leaves that can look a bit dull. As an evergreen tree, they really don't look very colourful for most of the year. The flowers come out to brighten our lives for a very short time in late Winter or early Spring. The flowers look like bright yellow fluffy balls but they don't last for very long. However, we know that next year they will come out again and we will smile.

Our lives can be like the Wattle tree, dull and boring for most of the time but there will be times, however short, when we will experience bright sunshiny moments. They won't last for long, but they will brighten our lives and help us smile. We can be sure that we will have other bright moments, just like the Wattle trees will have new flowers next year.

Of course, we won't necessarily have to wait a year, it may be a few days or a few weeks, but there will be bright moments ahead.

"But unto you, that fear my name shall the Sun of righteousness arise with healing in his wings, and ye shall go forth, and grow up as calves of the stall." Malachi 4:2

<u>Prayer:</u> Thank you, Lord, for the bright things you send to help us smile.

♆ 349

No amount of money will buy you some things in this life. Rain; it is such an important thing that keeps the plants and animals alive. God determines when and where it falls. He even decides how much we will get. Most days, even the weather man can only guess at when or how much rain will fall. Sunshine; it is necessary for plant growth and good mental health of humans.

There are some other things that money cannot buy; the faithfulness of a friend, yes, many will be friends while you have money, but when it runs out, so do they. Love; cannot be bought. The greatest gift of all, eternal life, can definitely not be purchased with money. It was paid for by the blood of Christ and is freely offered to the richest people, right down to the poorest, with the same amount of mercy.

> **"Being justified freely by his grace through the redemption that is in Christ Jesus:" Romans 3:24**

Challenge: Lord, help me to remember that money cannot buy me the most important things in life.

350

Have you ever noticed that the shadows of time are not quite true? If you look at the shadows of the hands on a clock, they are always a little bit out. If we want to know what the real time is, we must make sure that we are looking at the real thing, not the shadow.

The same could also be said of life. If you want to know what the truth is, we must look at the real source for our information. You don't get to know a person by listening to the rumours about them, you get true knowledge by meeting them, talking to them, and learning about them over a period of time.

So, when you want to know about Jesus, where do you go? The Bible, it's our source of true knowledge.

> **"For the word of God *is* quick, and powerful, and sharper than any two-edged sword, piercing even to the dividing asunder of soul and spirit, and of the joints and marrow, and *is* a discerner of the thoughts and intents of the heart." Hebrews 4:12.**

Prayer: Lord, I thank you that I can find out the truth about you through your word.

🍷 351

All geometric patterns start the same way. You have to have a few straight lines. Whether they are in the form of timber or pencil or some other medium, how they cross and join will determine how the pattern looks when it is finished.

As humans, we have all started off the same way. We are sinful, we have decided that we want to do things our way. This is a problem for God. He wants us to live the way that He knows is best. So, He came up with a geometric design of His own to help us get back to Him.

"Who his own self bare our sins in his own body on the tree, that we, being dead to sins, should live unto righteousness: by whose stripes ye were healed." 1 Peter 2:24

<u>Prayer:</u> Thank you, Lord, for making a way out of my eternal death through your son, Jesus Christ, by sending Him to die for me.

🍷 352

One year we decided to try Secret Santa as a way of managing our gift giving. Family members were finding it too expensive to give quality gifts to all members of the family. This way they would be able to buy something of value for one person.

Gift giving at Christmas time is supposed to remind us of God's gift of salvation which was given freely as an act of grace and undeserved by us. It was the costliest gift that God could have given us.

This gift was also essential for mankind. It is the only way we can have eternal life with God in Heaven. There is just no other way to have our relationship with God restored. Unless we accept this wonderful gift, we will be forever doomed to hell.

When we are preparing for Christmas, do we think about what the recipient needs and would like, or do we just get something so we look acceptable to others?

"For unto us a child is born, unto us a son is given: and the government shall be upon his shoulder: and his name shall be called Wonderful, Counsellor, The mighty God, The everlasting Father, The Prince of Peace."
Isaiah 9:6

Prayer: May I always be aware of just how much it cost you, Lord, to give me the gift of eternal life.

353

We all need to learn about the real meaning of Christmas. It seems that commercialisation of Christmas encourages those selfish desires in each of us that create disharmony and stress. There is so much advertising hype that makes people feel as if nothing is good enough. Advertisers continue to bombard us with messages to entice us to outdo everyone else.

That first Christmas was about so many unselfish acts. Mary accepted the miracle of carrying the Son of God regardless of what family and friends would think of her. In the society that Mary grew up in you could be killed for being a single mum, and who on earth was going to understand an immaculate conception. Joseph unselfishly put aside his feelings and desires to look after Mary and Jesus, again regardless of how weak and stupid he may have looked to others. In Bethlehem, the Inn Keeper unselfishly allowed Mary and Joseph to use the stable. It's hard to believe that this is a remarkable act, but if the Inns were arranged the way I understand them to be; with everyone sleeping on mats around the walls in the same room, then his willingness to arrange some form of privacy for her indicates to me that he was an unselfish man. The wise men travelled a great distance and gave gifts. Goodwill and Joy are born out of the unselfishness of humans towards each other.

"For you know the grace of our Lord Jesus Christ, that though He was rich, yet for your sake He became poor so that you through His poverty might become rich." 2 Corinthians 8:9.

Prayer: Lord, let me give more, so that people will see more of you.

🍷 354

A sign outside a shop or town will tell you where you are. There are signs on roads that tell you how far it is to the next destination. There are billboard signs that tell you all about places to visit. The speed limit sign reminds you of your legal obligation.

At Christmas time, we hang a wreath on our front door. Why do we use these things as decorations for Christmas? It seems that, in ancient Rome, people used decorative wreaths as a sign of victory. Some believe that this is where the hanging of wreaths on doors came from. According to my research, the origins of the Advent wreath can be found in the folk practices of the pre-Christian Germanic peoples who, during the cold December darkness of Eastern Europe, gathered wreaths of evergreen branches, and lighted fires as signs of hope in the coming spring and renewed light. Christians, it seems, kept these traditions alive, and by the 16th century, these symbols were used throughout Germany to celebrate their Advent hope in Christ, the everlasting Light.

"Thy sun shall no more go down; neither shall thy moon withdraw itself: for the LORD shall be thine everlasting light, and the days of thy mourning shall be ended." Isaiah 60:20.

So, I am happy to hang my wreath on my door even if it does have "bows" instead of candles. In my mind, the bows can represent the wrapping of a gift or even ribbons given as prizes for winning.

Prayer: I thank you God for giving us the very best gift two thousand years ago, Jesus Christ, who not only showed us how to live, but rose victorious after His death on the cross so that we can have the hope of eternal life.

355

I was thinking about why we use lots of red in our decorations at Christmas time. It is a reflection on the warmth that the colour conveys, the warmth of God's love that meant that he sent his Son down to earth to save mankind (John 3:16). Maybe it reflects the warmth of winter fires that burn in the Northern Hemisphere where many of our traditions come from, reminding us of the power of the Holy Spirit. It is to remind us of the blood that Jesus shed for us on the cross, the reason He came to earth in the first place.

Another colour that we see a lot of at Christmas time is white. This reflects the clean look that comes with snow that falls in those Northern winters and reminds us of the purity of Jesus because He has never committed a wrong deed.

Green, reflecting the evergreen trees, should prompt us to remember the everlasting faithfulness of God because:

"Jesus Christ is the same yesterday, today and forever." Hebrews 13:8.

Prayer: Lord, all the decorations we bring out at this time of year are to teach us to appreciate the love that you have for us. Help us to learn these lessons well.

356

If a decoration is an embellishment on a basic structure, it occurs to me that Christmas, to many people, could be considered a decoration on a year. We all plough through the struggles that life sends us from January to

November and then December arrives! I wonder if we don't see the parties, celebrations, and hype as a distraction from the mundane issues of life.

I understand that many people actually hate Christmas. This time of year brings out the worst of their fears, sorrows, insecurities, and anxieties, affecting their reactions to those around them.

The celebration of Christmas has had a chequered past, throughout history. There have been the extremes in what was an acceptable way to pass the festive season. During the reign of Oliver Cromwell, it would appear that there was to be no outward show of celebration and this was apparently in response to the over-indulgences of the previous years. As a child, I was led to believe that this was similar to the "over the top" commercialisation we see today.

Regardless of how we feel about Christmas, the truth is that, at the time when Jesus was born, there was no decoration. At that time two young people were going to be first-time parents. Yes, they knew that they were going to welcome a very special baby into the world but that happened under the roughest of conditions.

We have two accounts of the birth of Jesus and they can be read in Matthew 1:18-23 and Luke 1:1-2:20.

Prayer: Lord, help me to remember the simple truth about Christmas, that you came to earth to live, save us, and help us to reconnect with you.

357

Over the Christmas period, I have many conversations with the single parents that I know. There is one question that always seems to come up. "Where are the children spending Christmas?"

There are different responses, "their father's this year"; "it's their mother's turn", or "they will be with us this year". Sadly, there is often a comment that makes these situations sad and that is "it's the only time we get to see them".

As I reflected on these conversations, I thought of another father who only gets to see his children one or twice a year. Yes, that father is our Heavenly Father, God, who only see's so many of His children at Christmas or Easter. How many people believe that they only need to go to church at Christmas or Easter, for Weddings, Funerals, or Baptisms? So many, yet they are His children who He loves so dearly. There are many reasons given for not attending. Some don't care, some have been hurt so badly, and others just consider that there is no need to attend Church to have a relationship with God. Just like our earthly parents our Father God hurts when we ignore Him.

"Jerusalem, Jerusalem, you who kill the prophets and stone those sent to you, how often I have longed to gather your children together, as a hen gathers her chicks under her wings, and you were not willing." Luke 13:34 (NIV).

Challenge: Let us make sure that we stay connected with Jesus all year round.

358

I sat in church and I was so proud of my children because all of them had made an effort to attend, even though some of them consider the church to be full of faults and hypocrites. They had made the effort to travel home from the various places they live to make me happy, which it did, and as I looked at each of them in turn, children, and spouses, I knew a rush of pride for all of them. What they weren't to know though, was that as important this was to me, there was something else that was more important.

I stood singing Christmas Carols throughout the service, and with each hymn I remembered my mother waiting for all of us in Heaven. As I looked again at my family, my only prayer was that they too would go to Heaven. In order to do this, they need to look beyond the church and its faults, to God Himself and make that total commitment to Him, give their lives to His control.

Oh, I understand that they will have to make their own choices but my prayer is that all of them will make the choice that will see us all gathered together one day forever.

"And then shall he send his angels, and shall gather together his elect from the four winds, from the uttermost part of the earth to the uttermost part of heaven." Mark 13:27.

Prayer: Lord, I look forward to one day joining family and friends in Heaven with you.

359

Like every inquisitive child, I asked my parents to clarify why we have a tree at Christmas time. The explanation was simple. When God makes a promise, we can be very sure that He will keep it. It is a sure thing, always alive, just like the evergreen tree. Its leaves are always green; they don't turn brown and fall off, making the tree look lifeless during winter.

The shape as well, pointing upwards helping to remind us that Jesus has returned to Heaven, considered to be above the sky to young children. It also helps us remember that God promises to send Jesus back one day and we will have to look up into the sky when that happens. On the top of the tree, we place either a star or an angel recalling that Jesus' birth was announced by the star that travelled to Bethlehem or the host of angels that sang in the night sky to tell the shepherds to go and visit the new born king.

Of course, this is useless if, after Christmas is over, we don't continue to live the life that Christ came to earth to show us how to live.

"In Him was life, and the life was the Light of men." John 1:4.

Prayer: Lord Jesus, please fill me with your light that I might show others your goodness.

360

My husband and I are still renovating our home. We have been in this process for over twenty years now. As the children have all left home and there is just the two of us to finish some of the jobs, we need to work together. When we decided to add some fretwork to the archway between the kitchen and family room, we needed to get some pieces of wood to line up side by side. Unfortunately, I failed to see straight and some pieces ended up being a little out of line. However, as far as I'm concerned, the overall effect works well.

As we work side by side for the Lord, we will find that sometimes things don't line up quite as they should, or as well as we would like, but the Lord is the builder of His church and He will make sure that the overall effect is for His glory.

"So then neither is he that planteth anything, neither he that watereth; but God that giveth the increase." 1 Corinthians 3:7.

Challenge: To do my best and leave the rest up to God.

361

When we see certain types of clouds, we know that a storm is coming. There is nothing we can do to stop it. We cannot know how bad it will be, how long it will last, or how much damage it will do. All we can do is batten down anything that is going to get blown away in the wind, and wait.

In life, we also can see storms coming. Certain situations will always create a storm. It doesn't matter if it's a family get-together, illness, or a change in circumstances. We can see them coming and again, there is nothing we can do to stop them arriving.

The only thing we can do is put our trust in the one person who controls storms.

"And he saith unto them, Why are ye fearful, O ye of little faith? Then he arose and rebuked the winds and the sea, and there was a great calm."
Matthew 8:26.

Prayer: Lord, help me to remember that you are in control of everything and therefore, I don't need to be afraid of any of the storms of life.

362

I visited a church that I had had connections with many years ago. As I sat down, a feeling much like coming home washed over me. I contemplated that feeling and tried to work out what it really was because this church was not home, the home was in another town. Finally, I realized that it was like a child visiting a loved relative. This wasn't home but very close.

We are all family. Each branch has its different ways of doing things and God uses them to meet the needs of those around them.

As I joined in the singing, listened to the choir, the children's message and sermon, I was so blessed and spiritually refreshed and for that, I thank my Lord for bringing me to my home away from home even for just a short visit.

"So, we, *being* many, are one body in Christ, and every one members one of another." Romans 12:5

Prayer: Thank you, Lord, for my extended family that I have in You.

363

Once while I was visiting Sydney, I found a small house stuck between two larger buildings. It looked as if it could easily be squashed. I am sure that it once was just another house in a long line of terrace houses. It reminds people of what used to be - a great line of beautiful homes, full of family life.

Yet now, it's an old-fashioned house standing proudly amongst modern buildings.

As we read our Bible and history we come across so many situations where there were just a few Christians left, telling others the truth about God and His grace and mercy. They are like that house, small and squashed in the evil world around them.

Do you feel small and compressed in the world that we live in? This problem is not new, Paul had the same problem when he was alive.

"Am I, therefore, become your enemy, because I tell you the truth?" Galatians 4:16.

If you are feeling a little overwhelmed just because you hold to the truth, remember that God sees you, and loves you, and wants you to live for Him, not for the world around you.

Prayer: Lord, thank you that you will protect me, no matter how small and insignificant I feel in this world.

364

I went to the pantry cupboard the other day and discovered that there were two packets of Candy Canes left after Christmas. These sweets are made of strips of red, white, and sometimes green hard candy twisted together in a spiral pattern. Finally, they shaped to look like a walking cane or shepherd's crook before being packed for sale.

There is a story that says the original candy canes were made to remind all of us that; Jesus is our Shepherd who loves and cares for us and shed His blood (red) for us.

"I am the good shepherd: the good shepherd giveth his life for the sheep." John 10:11.

This means that he can take away our sins and present us as pure as snow (white) to His father on judgment day.

"In the body of his flesh through death, to present you holy and unblameable and unreproveable in his sight:" Colossians 1:22.

His promises and faithfulness are everlasting (green).

"Jesus Christ is the same yesterday and today and forever." Hebrews 13:8.

This sweet is made with hard candy to remind us that Jesus has a strength that is stronger than anything we know.

"I can do all things through Christ which strengtheneth me." Philippians 4:13.

So, when I look at the candy canes, I am reminded of how much Jesus loves us all and I remember what Isaiah 53:5 says:

"But he was wounded for our transgressions, *he was* bruised for our iniquities: the chastisement of our peace *was* upon him, and with his stripes, we are healed."

Prayer: Lord, what a wonderful way to remember how much you love every day.

♀ 365

As we head towards the end of each year, it is very common to look back over the things that have happened. Are you amazed that you are still standing? or are you flying high with great feelings of achievement and expectations met? At our stage in life, most of us, I suspect, will be walking a middle line between highs and lows.

As I read Philippians 4:10-19, I ask myself if Paul was writing this towards the end of a year. We know that it was written towards the end of his second imprisonment, and more than likely, his life, but I wondered if this letter might also have been written as part of Paul's evaluation of a year.

"In everything and in all things, I have learned the secret both to be filled and to be hungry, both to abound and to be in need. I can do all things through Christ, who strengthens me." Philippians 4:12b-13.

It's a letter of thanks for the assistance and prayers of those people living in Philippi. He is able to say, as he looks back, that he can see that God has been his strength and that God has been faithful, even when life has dished out its worst and served up its best.

As you look back over the year, do you ask God to show you where His hand has protected you, cared for you and held you back for your growth? When we do this consistently, we will be able to experience peace in all circumstances, just as Paul did.

Prayer: Heavenly Father, we thank you for the year that we have had. We thank you for your protection, lessons, and the way that you have helped us to grow closer to you. As we look forward to the next year Father, help us to remember your grace and move forward with a stronger confidence in your faithfulness.

One Last Glass

When it comes to viewing the skyline from my house, I am absolutely spoilt for choice. As I walk around my house, I can stop at any point and see mountains, the valley, trees, and a vast sky that goes on forever.

God has definitely been there for me this year. As each hollow and mountain have been moved through or climbed, He has proven that He has the answers worked out well in advance. He has sent the right person at the right time or just given me the energy, motivation, and strength, to get through the list of things to be carried out.

So, no matter where I look, I see the mountains and I am reminded that God not only made these wonderful formations, but He will care for me. He cares for me, a very small speck of that great creation.

"I will lift up mine eyes unto the hills from whence cometh my help. My help cometh from the Lord, which made heaven and earth. He will not suffer thy foot to be moved he that keepeth thee will not slumber. Behold he that keepeth Israel shall neither slumber nor sleep. The Lord is thy keeper: The Lord is thy shade upon thy right hand. The sun shall not smite thee by day nor the moon by night. The Lord shall preserve thee from all evil he shall preserve thy soul. The Lord shall preserve thy going out and thy coming in from this time forth and even for evermore."
Psalm 121

Prayer: Lord, as I look forward to the New Year, I know that those mountains prove God's faithfulness.

Other Books by this Author
All these books are available as eBooks

Turning Water into Wine – 2nd Edition
100 Stories of God's Hand in Life

More Water into Wine, 2nd Edition
100 Stories of God's Hand in Life

Still More Water into Wine
100 Stories of God's Hand in Life

Reflections
Australian Stories from my Father's Past

Conversations with Myself – Volume 1
100 Stories of Hope, Faith and Determination

Whispers from on High
Poetry and short stories.

Follow Helen Brown on:
Facebook: https://www.facebook.com/HelenBrownCollection/

Instagram: https://www.instagram.com/helen_brown_books/

Pinterest: https://www.pinterest.com.au/helenbrown58726/

www.ingramcontent.com/pod-product-compliance
Lightning Source LLC
Chambersburg PA
CBHW030253010526
44107CB00053B/1692